How China Made It

The road from agrarian poverty to manufacturing dominance

Martin Lynch

How China Made It: The road from agrarian poverty to manufacturing dominance

ISBN: 978-1-922460-98-1 (paperback)

Published in Australia by Martin Lynch and InHouse Publishing.
www.inhousepublishing.com.au

Printed in Australia by InHouse Print & Design.

INHOUSE PTY LTD PUBLISHING

NATIONAL LIBRARY OF AUSTRALIA

A catalogue record for this book is available from the National Library of Australia

Contents

Introduction

The economic rise of China is the most important global geopolitical development since the collapse of the Soviet Union. This being the case, it is useful to have a good understanding of the path that China followed in achieving its economic success. The aim of this book is to make a contribution to that understanding. It is the first in a four-part series which examines the progress of global industrial development and the impact of that development on the global mining industry.

China's path from poverty to the world's largest economy was not the result of a carefully calculated series of reforms. It is much more accurate to describe it in the words of Deng Xiaoping: China made the journey from poverty to wealth by "crossing the river by feeling for the stones". It was a journey with a clear destination but only a hazy notion of how to get there. There were some policy initiatives which were outright failures, and the benefits that the most successful of them delivered came mostly from unintended consequences. It helped that China was in the right place at a time when the rules of international trade were changing fundamentally. The biggest contribution of the country's leadership was to adapt quickly to unforeseen circumstances and take full advantage of the opportunities which fell into their lap.

There are five chapters.

Chapter 1 deals with the Mao years, which are important because they laid the foundations, both strong and weak, on which the reform era was built.

Chapter 2 deals with the 1980s, which was the first decade of the reform era and the decade in which reform activity was at its height. Three important reforms were enacted. One of them, the dissolution of the Agricultural Communes, had an immediate impact and its ramifications drove the Chinese economy through the rest of the decade. The next reform, the establishment of the Special Economic Zones, was a partial success in the 1980s, but its real impact came in the following decade. The third reform was an attempt to make the city-based state-owned enterprises more competitive and more entrepreneurial. This was a failure, and the ill-feeling it created was a significant contributor to social unrest which led up to the Tienanmen Square massacre of 1989, or the June 4 Incident as it is known in China.

Chapter 3 deals with the 1990s. This decade started with a tense stand-off between the conservatives and the reformers, which was only resolved when Deng Xiaoping embarked on his famous Southern Tour. China was back in economic growth mode by 1992 and the rest of the decade was a prosperous time. The Special Economic Zones took-off, helped along by the shift of Hong Kong and Taiwan's manufacturing sectors over to the mainland. The result was that the export sector became the engine of the economy. The big reform effort of this decade was a second attempt at making the state-owned enterprises more competitive as businesses. This time it was even more ambitious and far-reaching, and it was successful. One part of it involved the privatisation of government-owned housing. Unbeknownst to the reformers, their creation of widespread home ownership was to become the prime mover of the economy in the next decade.

Chapter 4 deals with the two decades from 2000 to 2020. In the first ten years, the Chinese economy went from being virtually unknown around the world to being a talking point in every western workplace. It was a golden decade for China, driven by an urban construction boom and an unusually free global market for trade in cheap, reasonable-quality manufactured goods – a market in which China became the undisputed king. The second decade saw all of this progressively come off the boil as the Global Financial Crisis in the western economies slowed the export engine, and the construction boom reached a plateau.

Chapter 5 looks at the coming decade. The great successes of the past 40 years were due in large part to the willingness of its leadership to make bold reforms and then fully capitalise on the often-unintended benefits which flowed from them. These benefits continued to flow well after the reform process slowed to a stop. But the country cannot live off its past efforts forever. The last important reform was made 19 years ago. Unless the reform process is brought back to life – and there is plenty still to be done - it may well be that the once-unstoppable China becomes just another middle income country, its economic growth slowed by the headwinds of an aging population, a shrinking workforce, the withdrawal of international support and a leadership which places more importance on locking-down its people than on unlocking their potential.

Chapter 1

THE MAO ERA

The Starting Point

If China's journey from poverty to the world's largest economy can be said to have a distinct beginning in time, then it began in Beijing in December 1978,[1] during a five-day conference of the top leadership of the Chinese Communist Party. At that conference, China's senior leaders decided to abandon the Mao era emphasis on the raising the political awareness of the people. They instead resolved to focus their efforts on raising the living standards of the people.

Raising the living standards of the common people was always supposed to have been the focus of the Communists. It had been a big part of Chairman Mao's speech when, on an October afternoon in 1949, he stood in Tiananmen Square, in front of a rain-soaked crowd of 300,000 people, and claimed power over all China. But over the next three decades the Communists did not achieve too much by way of raising living standards. Each time genuine progress began to take place, a political upheaval, unleashed by Chairman Mao himself, would derail it and set things back a long way. Perhaps as many as twenty years of economic progress were sacrificed to his schemes. Such was his destructive influence that, had the Great Helmsman decided to retire after his speech on that rainy afternoon, the Chinese economy of 2020 may well have been achieved by the early 2000s.

To understand the state of the Chinese economy as it began its renaissance in 1978, it is necessary to trace the path of progress and upheaval that China went through in the thirty years which followed the coming to power of the Communist Party in 1949.

The First Five Year Plan

When the Communists came to power in China, it was a nation of impoverished peasant farmers. Seventy years of foreign domination and exploitation had been followed by thirty years of civil war and five years of murderous Japanese occupation. It had left the country in a mess. Most households were living on the bare minimum, and many were on the verge of starvation.

On the world stage, China, with at least one fifth of the world's population, mattered little in terms of military might. As a centre of manufacturing, it mattered even less. To take just one measure: during 1949 the war-ravaged country produced 158,000 tonnes of steel.[2] That same year, the United States produced 70 million tonnes.

The most pressing challenge facing the Communists in 1949 was to help the nation feed itself. So the first step was nation-wide land reform. Farming land was taken from the landlords and wealthy farming families and given to the poor farmers and landless peasants who had supported the Communists in their 25-year struggle. This move provided the hoped-for impetus to Chinese grain production and by 1952 the food situation was strong enough to allow Mao and the rest of the Party leadership to turn their attention to building the industrial base.

The main pockets of industry were in Manchuria, the name given to China's three northern-most coastal provinces, and in Shanghai, which had long been China's main commercial city. Much of the industrial capacity had been destroyed during the civil war and Japanese occupation, but in truth there had not been much to start with.

There was debate as to how the re-building and expansion of this industrial base should be done. The first question was: who should have control over the levers of industry? Some pointed to the Japanese post-war model, where private ownership and initiative was permitted within the confines of government direction. This was not a new concept in China. In fact, in the early 1950s most Chinese businesses and nearly all of its farms were still held in private ownership.

There was an alternative to private ownership with government guidance, and that was the Soviet model. Under this model, the government owned and controlled virtually all economic activity – including industry, farms and even retail shops. Private ownership had almost disappeared in the Soviet Union.

A second question was the style of industry on which to focus. Light or heavy? Light industry, such as the labour-intensive manufacture of textiles, furniture and small consumer items, would be a lower cost pathway to industrialization, would be faster to develop and be a better fit with China's masses of semi-employed, semi-literate farm workers. But a focus on heavy industry also had attractions. The construction of steel mills, electrical power plants, chemical and fertilizer factories and large machinery workshops would deliver a national industrial base which could be used to support all manner of industrial, and military, development in the future.

The decision eventually was made to go down the path of heavy industry and government ownership and control. The reasoning went that allowing private owners to take the lead in national development risked inviting back the very forms of exploitation which the Communists had spent decades trying to defeat. The choice in favour of heavy industry was made because it would help strengthen the country's military defences. It was a time when the Korean War was still raging and the US army was on the country's doorstep. Added to that, Chiang Kai-shek and his Nationalist army which had fought the Communists during the thirty-year civil war were defeated but still posed a threat. They were firmly entrenched in Taiwan, just two hundred kilometres off the coast of China.

The next question was: how to get started with this government-controlled nation-wide program of heavy industrial development? This was easy enough to answer, because a roadmap already existed. Beginning in the late 1920s, the Soviet Union had done just what China now intended to do. They had built a large heavy industry base in a vast, agrarian, poorly-educated and poverty-stricken country. They had done it via a series of Five Year Plans which had focused on the building of "mega-projects" – huge industrial and infrastructure works which employed tens of thousands and served as the focal point of entire cities.

So it was that in 1953, borrowing from the model pioneered by Joseph Stalin, China's first Five Year Plan was launched. It called for the construction of coal mines, steel works, power stations, fertilizer plants, tractor factories and a whole range of heavy machinery manufacturing complexes. The aim was to double, in five years, the output of coal, electricity, fertilisers and machine tools. As for steel, the Plan called for a fourfold increase. The idea was that it would all be achieved through the construction of mega-projects. There were nearly 600 of them in the Plan, of which 150 would be led by Soviet engineers. To make it all happen, an army of Chinese bureaucrats was recruited to devise an all-encompassing, nation-wide labour and raw material distribution plan which would govern the whole effort.

As it turned out, the first Five Year Plan was a huge success. By 1957 China's industrial landscape had been transformed. The old Anshan steel mill in Manchuria had been expanded and rejuvenated as were China's two other existing mills, one in Shanghai and the other in Beijing. Three other steel mills were in an advanced state of construction. Dams, bridges, underground coal mines, iron ore quarries, a dozen power stations, several fertilizer plants, two tractor plants and a whole raft of other industrial works had come into operation. Virtually all the Plan targets had been achieved.[3]

The Communists had been busy in other areas too. Private business had all but disappeared. Agriculture also had been taken over by the government. Where once there had been the family farm, by 1957 there was the Agricultural Collective.[4] This was, in essence, an industrial farm, formed by pooling the land, labour and equipment of 50 to 100 families. The idea behind the Collectives was that they could achieve much greater grain production per hectare. This would come about because larger fields were easier to work, and larger farms could afford to use tractors. The peasants had the right to withdraw from them, at least on paper. But withdrawals were not expected. Confidence was high that the Collectives would dramatically increase grain production.

The Great Leap Forward

Despite the great successes, Mao Zedong had been unimpressed with the achievements of the first Five Year Plan. He saw that the technicians and labourers working in the mega-projects had enjoyed an improvement in living standards but the peasants had not. He determined that the next Five Year Plan would focus on raising the standard of living of the peasant farmers and their families.

Mao was not alone in wanting this. Many in the Communist Party felt the same way. But there was no agreement on how to do it. Chen Yun, the Party's chief planner, thought the answer lay in relaxing the government control of agriculture and allowing a return to the free market at the farm level. Mao had a different view. He thought that the solution lay in giving the peasants more responsibility for the industrial side of the economy as well as the agricultural side. For this to work, the peasants would have to be organised into groups large enough to be able to deal with both industrial and agricultural production.

The newly-formed Agricultural Collectives were considered for this role, but they were too small. Someone came up with the idea of combining the Collectives into even larger organisations.[5] They proposed the formation of huge Communal Farms consisting of up to 30,000 people. Because they would have such a large population, it was assumed that somewhere within each of the Communes would be found people capable of building iron-making furnaces, coal mines and tool-making workshops. It was further assumed that there would be people experienced in mining, so that iron ore and coal pits could be found and dug to feed these furnaces. Then those same people, or others, could fashion the steel they produced into farming implements and simple machinery. It was not just steel which would be produced by the peasants. Cement for construction, coal for heating and fertilisers for crops would all be produced in peasant-built facilities. Mao liked the idea.

The beauty of this scheme was that it tackled two genuine challenges which had always faced the Chinese economy. One was the chronic underemployment of the peasants, the other was transport. Outside of harvest and sowing times, the peasants had little to do. They were a vast wasted resource. The Communes would eliminate this waste by putting the peasants to work in mines and factories when they were not working in the fields. As for the problem of transport, getting materials from one place to another was an everpresent problem in a country as large as China. The Communes would eliminate this because they would produce everything themselves.

Once the Communes were established, and the right to withdraw from them had been taken away, the second Five Year Plan was ready to go. The targets were set by the senior leadership in Beijing. They decreed that the national grain harvest would triple in size over the next five years and that the national industrial output would increase fivefold. Exactly how to achieve it was left up to the Communes. The assumption was that the neglected and underestimated peasants would respond magnificently to the challenge, and bear the country aloft and carry it into the industrial age. And they would do it all without the arrogant Russian engineers with their mega-projects.

When Mao spoke of his vision of this highly productive peasant paradise, it sounded like it might work. The broader leadership Communist Party was not so sure. But what Mao wanted, he generally got. So it was that, in 1958, the Second Five Year Plan was launched. It was, to say the least, an extraordinarily ambitious set of targets. It came to be known as the Great Leap Forward.[6]

From this distance in time, the Great Leap Forward has all the hallmarks of an enterprise doomed to failure. This is because it depended on three things all working out well, each of which was very unlikely in itself. Firstly, it depended upon China's legions of peasant farmers producing far more grain by grouping themselves into small armies without having any professional management to control their new organisations. Secondly, it depended on that same army of poorly-coordinated peasants building and operating metallurgical and chemical processes in which they had no experience and only the most basic training. Thirdly, it relied on those same peasants then using this home-made steel, cement and other materials to create complex machinery and engineering works.

So how did it go? In the first year, things went remarkably well. There was a good harvest in 1958. Rivers of pig iron flowed from the multitude of new furnaces which sprang up throughout the farming regions of China. Cement, fertilisers and other basic raw materials were produced with similar gusto. Coal production showed a true leap forward – it doubled in a single year. This was indeed quite an achievement because China was already a coal producer of global significance. So, as the first year of the Great Leap Forward came to a close it seemed that Mao had been right. Peasant labour, properly harnessed, looked like it may well be able to propel China to the status of a major industrial power far quicker than anyone thought possible. But 1958 was as good as it got.

As 1959 dawned, it was clear to many that the Communes were under severe stress. Peng Dehuai, a senior military man and also the Defence Minister, spoke publicly of the problems looming. In response Mao removed him and his allies from their positions. Unfortunately, ignoring the problem did not solve it. The crops failed in 1959, and the mountains of peasant steel proved useless. This was despite the fact that, in some instances, perfectly good ploughs and tractor bodies were hacked up and melted down to boost the output. Grain shortages quickly followed, compounded by the fact that rural officials, frightened of retribution from Beijing, had overstated grain production, which led Beijing-based officials to requisition more of it, storing it in city warehouses, far away from where it was needed.

The grain shortages were made worse by the Four Pests Campaign.[7] Not content with requiring the peasants to make steel and cement as well as greatly increasing the harvest, Mao also asked them to rid the countryside of the nation's four pests – rats, flies, mosquitoes and sparrows. Why sparrows? Because they ate the grain. Overlooked was the fact that the sparrows also ate the locusts which would otherwise devour the grain. The anti-sparrow campaign worked, and the resultant surge in the locust population wrought additional havoc on the harvest.

By year's end, these realities had filtered through to the upper levels of government in Beijing, and even Mao was admitting failure. Yet the carnage was not over. The next year drought struck and the crops failed again, this time catastrophically. Famine was the consequence. Another blow came in May 1960 when Nikita Krushchev, President of the Soviet Union, exasperated at the way the good work of the first Five Year Plan was being squandered, withdrew all of the Russian engineers. In a stroke the country lost many of its most experienced technical people. The Great Leap Forward was abandoned in June 1960.

The following year the chickens really came home to roost. Industrial output collapsed and the famine deepened. It gripped most of China and, in the next few years, between twenty and fifty million people would die of starvation, disease and exhaustion.[8] Most of the mines and furnaces built by the Communes stopped functioning as their exhausted and malnourished workers gave up on them. Mao, bearing the blame, lost his influence and his job as Chairman of the People's Republic. Others would assume the task of picking up the pieces and getting China back on its feet.

The Recovery

The failure of the Great Leap Forward was the first serious crisis to confront the Chinese Communist Party since 1949. It was a radical set of policies based upon an ideological view of what could be achieved by the working man. Whilst it did draw strong support at the time from many senior Party members, much of that support was probably given out of a preparedness to take a chance on Mao's vision and willpower. After all, his leadership had carried them through before. It had been a big factor in the Communists beating overwhelming opposition and rising to claim ultimate political power in China.

However, when it became clear that Mao's policies had failed, his aura of invincibility faded. Even his supporters began to cast about for new answers. In this way, Liu Shaoqi and Deng Xiaoping, assisted by Chen Yun, Zhou Enlai and others, took over the reins of economic management, nudging (as gently as possible) the hyper-egoistic Mao off to one side.[9]

It is fair to describe Liu and Deng as authoritarian Chinese nationalists, as opposed to committed Communists.[10] They were both strong supporters of the Communist Party and its right to rule over China. That said, they often supported economic policies which were not in keeping with the accepted Communist doctrine. They were not alone in this. Many Chinese communists were fighting not for a communist utopia but for Chinese independence and self-sufficiency. They joined the Communist party because in its policies and organisation they recognized a good vehicle for achieving their aims. They were pragmatists when it came to economic policies. Their approach is well-expressed by a quote attributed to Deng Xiaoping in 1961: "It doesn't matter whether the cat is black or yellow. As long as it catches mice it is a good cat."[11] (In the modern version of that quote, the non-black cat is white.)

This flexible approach to economic policy was accompanied by an inflexible commitment to maintaining the Party's political authority and military power. Like most senior members of the Party, both Liu and Deng had decades of experience in military leadership in difficult circumstances. Liu had helped lead the Communist resistance to the invading Japanese during the darkest years of the

1930s. He then led the Communist forces in northern China as they battled Chiang Kai-shek's army in the years after World War II. As for Deng Xiaoping, he had worked in the role of political organizer at the height of the civil war, and had participated in the Long March, the Communist Party's epic 7,000 kilometre retreat across China in the mid 1930s. Whilst he appears benign in comparison to Mao, Deng was a hard man. Mao had put him in charge of suppressing resistance in Tibet and the south-west provinces. He was also given responsibility for crushing dissenters in the mid-1950s when Mao's "let a hundred flowers bloom" declaration had unleashed a lot more dissent than he bargained for.

The most pressing task facing Liu and Deng was to restore the harvest and end the famine. Above all, fertilisers were needed. They began by importing it from Japan and Germany, but this was a short-term fix while they set about expanding and modernizing the domestic fertiliser production base. The Russians were gone, and along with them their industrial designs. So, for the first time in fifty years western companies were invited in to provide technical support and project management. Several European firms were commissioned to design and oversee the construction of eight modern nitrate and phosphate fertiliser plants.

Farm equipment was also needed. The manufacture of tractors received priority as did irrigation equipment such as pumps. The factories manufacturing them received steel shipments as a matter of priority. Along with steel, cement was needed. Quarries and kilns were built throughout the country, supplying cement for a vast number of local irrigation projects including wells, weirs and water distribution channels.[12]

Armaments factories and other industrial facilities which were not useful for agriculture were shuttered. This made available millions of city-based factory workers to be sent to the farms. Legions of city-born youth accompanied them, seeing the countryside for the first time.

To produce at their best, the farm workers needed more than just the bare minimum living conditions. They needed adequate footwear, warm clothes and at least some household comforts. The first Five Year Plan had downplayed the need for such things, and during the Great Leap Forward there had been no time for them. But Deng and Liu recognized that something had to be done to raise morale. So the long-neglected consumer goods sector received an injection of funds. For the first time since the Communists took power, consumer goods factories across China attracted more funding than the heavy industrial projects.

The harvests began to improve. By 1965 grain production was back to the level of 1958. Yet the country was still very poor. Casting about for a faster track for national development, Liu and Deng would have learnt all about the economic miracle which was at that time transforming Japan. That country's industrial base had been destroyed during the war, yet it was now producing three times more steel and cement than China. The Japanese did have an advantage in that they were rebuilding, not industrialising for the first time as was the case in China. Nevertheless, it would have occurred to Liu and Deng that the Japanese model of state-supported, trade-focussed industrial companies using western technology might work well in China. But the path was not yet clear for such a policy shift, because a formidable obstacle stood in the way. Mao Zedong, simmering on the sidelines, wanted his old job back.

The Cultural Revolution[13]

While most of the country saw Liu and Deng steering the economy back to a degree of prosperity, Mao saw something quite different. In his eyes, or so he claimed, the country was drifting back to behaviours of the past. Capitalism was creeping back in. The revolution was being lost and something drastic had to be done to defend it.

Mao had little support within the Communist Party upper echelons, who now saw him as a destabilizing force. So, in order to advance his cause, he began to engage in the same style of political agitation which had seen him take control of the Communist Party in the 1930s. His message to the masses was that China was once again falling prey to capitalists and foreign exploiters. He expertly fanned the flames of this fear campaign.

Then came the 1966 Communist Party Congress.[14] Mao crafted his Congress speech to appeal to the students and the workers. He called for a Great Proletarian Cultural Revolution to rid China of those who would drag the country back to the old days of oppressive capitalism and Confucian stagnation. He demanded the establishment of a body of guardians to protect this Cultural Revolution. They came to be known as the Red Guards.

The Cultural Revolution swept China with surprising speed. Such was Mao's popularity – he was regarded by many as having saved the country from western vultures and Japanese murderers - that his calls to arms were answered by tens of thousands, then hundreds of thousands, of students, workers and eventually soldiers. In August of 1966, over one million Red Guards packed into Tiananmen Square to rally in favour of Mao and his anti-capitalist crusade. The Guards were given licence to harass, beat and even kill anyone who they deemed to be a counter revolutionary.

Chaos and terror gripped the cities, and then spread into the farming areas. Many high-ranking officials fell victim. Factory managers were thrown out of their offices, to be replaced by Maoist zealots who had no idea of how to manage an actual industrial concern. Universities were closed down. In their place came the daily political indoctrination session. These sessions were devoted to fervent speeches spouting the latest Maoist line, and to studying Communist texts, prominent among them being a book of Chairman Mao's quotations. Due to its red cover, it came to be known outside China as the *Little Red Book*.

It was inevitable that Liu and Deng would be swept up in all this. They shared with Mao a belief in the supremacy of the Party, but they differed when it came to economic management. Mao's stated position was that revolutionary fervour was sufficient qualification for factory management, and that rewards for performance undermined the revolution. Liu and Deng believed in developing well-trained and technically-skilled managers, and rewarding good performance. Because of this, both were accused of "capitalist tendencies" and sent off to the countryside for re-education.

Liu had personally offended Mao and he suffered the full measure of revenge, eventually dying of his ill-treatment. Deng was a more adroit politician. He was close to Zhou Enlai, and Mao was always mindful that he might need someone with the skills of Deng once he was back in power. As a result, Deng's treatment was relatively mild, being limited to house arrest in a rural part of Jiangxi province. He was supposed to work in the local tractor factory but in fact spent most of his time writing and discussing politics.[15]

Deng's treatment raises a broader issue which helps explain why China was able to achieve so much so rapidly after Mao died. Mao's method of dealing with the people who challenged him was to send them off for re-education. Often they were later brought back, suitably chastened but with their talents still available. If China had been ruled by a character like Josef Stalin, the outstanding leadership group which led China through the first decades of the reform era would all have been dead by 1970. It is a big factor in explaining why the Communist Soviet Union collapsed while Communist China flourished.

After a few years of revolutionary mayhem, Mao was firmly back in the driver's seat in Beijing. Once there, he ordered the army to disperse the Red Guards, they no longer served his purpose. Peace returned to the streets but the fear and intimidation created by the violence remained. So too did the daily political indoctrination sessions. Time consuming and pointless, these sessions succeeded only in creating a timid and brow-beaten workforce, afraid to take any initiative.

The first years of the Cultural Revolution played havoc with the economy. Grain output fell and factories struggled to make their quotas. But the essential work continued to be done despite the wreckage being perpetrated in the name of protecting the revolution. When Mao finally called a stop to the violence, the economy rebounded and was soon growing at a healthy rate. For this to happen spontaneously, in the absence of any economic leadership, showed the underlying potential within China. It was a positive sign for the future.

Through the 1970s, Chairman Mao and the Party leadership progressively stepped back from the policies of the Cultural Revolution. In 1972, they hosted the visit of the President of the United States, Richard Nixon. Two years later, Deng Xiaoping was called back from exile, in part to provide a counter-weight to the Maoist hardliners who were by then stacked into the ranks of the Party leadership. A struggle ensued between Deng and his allies, on one side, and the Maoists on the other. The struggle intensified when the ultra-hardline Gang of Four emerged in the twilight of Mao's life. By 1976 they had gained enough influence to push Deng once again to the sidelines.

But their ascendancy was a brief one. Chairman Mao died later that year. Without his protection the Gang of Four stood no chance. Everyone else – the army, the bureaucracy and the rest of the Party leadership - was against them. The rejection of the Gang of Four was also an unspoken rejection of Mao's policies. China was on the verge of a big shift in its economic direction.[16]

Chapter 2

THE 1980s

Turning the Ship

Mao's passing brought to an end the first era of the Communist Party's leadership of the Chinese economy. Had the living standards of the Chinese people improved during that time?

To determine this, a baseline is needed. The Communists came to power in 1949 but because of the ruined state of the economy in that year, a better baseline to use is 1953. So the question is: had the average Chinese seen life improve between 1953, the year that the first Five Year Plan was launched, and 1976, the year of Mao's death?

If GDP is used as the measure, the answer is a qualified yes. The Communists had managed a respectable 4% annual increase over the period. If GDP *per person* is used as the measure, the progress was not particularly impressive. The economy had improved, but only at the rate of about 2% per year. This was slightly better than the average performance among the poor countries of the world at that time. But only slightly. In terms of GDP per person, China had climbed from ranking 140th in the world in 1953 to 135th in 1976. In that year it sat just below India, and just above war-torn Vietnam. It was far behind its East Asian neighbour and regional rival, Japan.

But GDP – whether total or per person - was not a measure which meant anything to the common people. What they wanted was enough to eat and a secure future for themselves and their children.

On the measure of how much there was to eat, total Chinese grain production had doubled between 1953 and 1976. But on the measure of total grain production *per person* only very modest gains had been made, all of which happened in the early years.[17] Between 1957 and 1976 grain production per person had not increased at all. And in any case, it was never enough. Hunger was an everpresent reality for many Chinese.

The food problem was not the only issue creating tensions in Chinese society. So too was the persistent lack of improvement in living standards. The average Chinese had seen virtually no improvement in their stock of material possessions since the early years of the 1950s. The focus had always been on investment in heavy industry and infrastructure. While there had been some periods of thaw in this policy, over the last twenty years consumer goods had always been in short supply.

Housing conditions had fared no better. Once again, there had been little change in 25 years. In 1980, the average floorspace per person in the cities was about five square metres, hardly different from the early 1950s.[18] Most families shared cooking, toilet and washing facilities with a group of other families. In about one third of apartments, two families lived together in a single room.

Yet hunger, cramped living conditions and shortages of warm clothing were not the worst of it. What was really trying the patience of the common people was the Cultural Revolution. The mob violence and arbitrary arrests had largely ended, although they were still a part of life. What remained in full force was the bullying and harassment towards anyone who was not sufficiently zealous in the endless indoctrination sessions. Of this, the common people had truly had enough. The Communist Party was failing them on food and living standards, and it was adding insult to injury by insisting they proclaim how effective the Party had been in furthering their welfare.

This message of discontent had got through to those seeking to take the reins in the post-Mao era. Everyone agreed that China had to get back on the path of economic progress and away from the struggles over ideological purity. There was disagreement, however, about which economic path to get onto.

One camp, led by Mao's anointed successor, Hua Guofeng, advocated increasing the focus on heavy industry and staying true to Mao's economic policy aims. Hua expressed it like this in a 1977 newspaper editorial: "We will resolutely uphold whatever policy decisions Chairman Mao made, and unswervingly follow whatever instructions Chairman Mao gave." It came to be known as the Two Whatevers.[19] To this end Hua released in early 1978 a Ten Year Plan which targeted big increases in industrial capacity, agricultural productivity and military capability. On the industrial front, ten new steel mills were proposed, including a giant integrated works in Shanghai, and another in Wuhan. It was an ambitious plan.

The opposing camp within the Party leadership wanted a different direction entirely. For them, Hua's Ten Year Plan[20] was a potentially ruinous re-run of the Great Leap Forward. The amount of money needed for the steelworks and all the other projects would cripple China and stretch to breaking point the patience of the people. Deng Xiaoping, now second in the Party hierarchy, was a leading voice in this camp. He was a popular figure and his clear manner of speaking appealed to many. According to him, the country needed a modest and achievable set of targets laid out in a Five Year Plan. The focus should be on increasing the harvest, building more apartments and producing more warm clothes. If anything, investment in heavy industry should be scaled back.

Hua was the man with the grand plan in 1978. But in the power struggle with Deng he was comprehensively outplayed. There could be no clearer indication of that than at the conference of the Chinese Communist Party leadership in December when his Ten Year Plan was officially rejected. To take its place, a new Five Year Plan was announced in April 1979. This extract from it summarises the new approach: "stress is placed on speeding up development of agriculture and the ... textile industries and on expanding production and construction in coal, petroleum, electrical power and building material industries, and in transport services". In other words, feeding, clothing and housing the people was to be the priority. Steel was not even on the list.

Just as the first era of Communist leadership was dominated by Mao Zedong, the second era came to be dominated by Deng Xiaoping. Deng was surely one of the greatest political leaders of the twentieth century, but he never at any time had a plan for reforming China. Instead, he had two core beliefs: the government had to put top priority on improving people's living conditions, and the Communist Party had to maintain its hold on the government. To achieve those ends, he was open to ideas. His greatest strength, as it turned out, was his ability to keep the Communist Party conservatives and central planners a safe distance away while the common people improved their living conditions for themselves.

The December 1978 conference recognised him as the real successor to Chairman Mao and elevated him to the position of China's "paramount leader". Whilst he set the tone and overall approach, he had two lieutenants who put that approach into practical effect. One of them was Hu Yaobang, a long-time comrade-in-arms. The other was Zhao Ziyang, an innovative economic reformer. Deng, Hu and Zhao formed the core of the group which led the great free market reforms of the coming decade.

They did not have the field all to themselves. Mao had died but many of the veterans who had fought alongside him were still very active in politics. Chen Yun, Li Xiannian, Bo Yibo, Yang Shangkun and others formed what was in effect a review panel of elder statesmen. They supported economic reforms aimed at raising living standards. They were conservatives, however, in that they ranked the goals of social stability and income equality above the goal of economic progress. If the two sets of goals conflicted, they would likely come down on the side of stability and equality.

Deng and his allies saw things differently. To them economic progress was the only way to maintain social stability. And to them income equality was not a worthwhile goal if it simply meant that living standards for everyone stayed low. Better to have some grow rich faster than others as long as the end result was that everyone grew richer.

During the first half of 1979 there were a lot of discussions aimed at bridging the gap between these two camps, and eventually a compromise course of action was agreed upon. This new course was confirmed at the national Party conference of September 1979, when two momentous decisions were made. One was to impose the One Child Policy, which restricted every Chinese family to having just one child. The other was to ratify the policy which was formally known as the Decision of the Central Committee of the Communist Party of China on the Question of Speeding Up Agricultural Development. It heralded sweeping reform in China's farming sector.

The Agricultural Revolution

It was no accident that the two big policy announcements of the September 1979 conference were both aimed at the problem of China's inadequate harvest. It was considered the most urgent of all the problems facing the new leadership. It is also no accident that both were announced at the same time.

Of the two new policies, the One Child Policy[21] had received by far the most study and debate. It was born out of the fact China's population was rising so fast that even good increases in the total grain output did little to improve the much more important measure of grain output per person. The Party leadership was well aware of this, and through the 1970s it had debated what should be done.

It was a difficult issue because the lack of improvement in grain output per person was not really due to the country's birth rate. The birth rate had been falling for twenty years. Instead the real "problem" was that at the same time as the birth rate was falling, infant mortality was also falling, and people were living longer. The authorities could hardly enact policies to increase infant mortality. Nor could they take steps to reduce life expectancy. So to stop the population from increasing at too fast a rate, the only course of action was to reduce the birth rate even further. It was not a popular decision amongst the common people, which is why the Party leadership had held back for so long. It is also why they announced the other policy at the same time.

To remind the reader, this other policy had the rather lengthy title of "Decision of the Central Committee of the Communist Party of China on the Question of Speeding Up Agricultural Development".[22] Essentially, it was a decision to consider breaking up the Agricultural Communes. In contrast to the unpopularity of the One Child Policy, the Party knew that this announcement would receive a warm welcome from the common people.

The Agricultural Communes still dominated the farm sector in 1979. They had never been popular. The once-independent farmers had lost their freedom, their individuality and any reward for effort. Because of this, as the 1970s wore on, the system had begun to fray at the edges. Here and there throughout China could be found Communes which had quietly split themselves into hundreds of much smaller work groups, and the authorities quietly allowed these individual groups to take responsibility for organizing their own lives and work practices. The model varied but in general the individual groups were obliged to give a pre-determined quantity of grain to the Commune, after that whatever surplus they produced they could use and sell as they saw fit.

The practice was called *baochan daozu*.[23] Although illegal, this reintroduction of incentives for effort – almost absent from Chinese farming for twenty years – was known to have a beneficial impact on the harvest. As a result, as time went on, increasingly there could be found senior Party officials who were prepared to publicly support it. One of the strongest supporters was Zhao Ziyang, who was then the Party Secretary in Sichuan Province. Another was, Wan Li, Party Secretary in Anhui Province. With these two provinces as strongholds, the practice spread without fanfare across China.

By 1978 Deng Xiaoping was also a supporter of the practice and he brought with him the conservatives, which is why a study into it was announced at the Party conference in December of that year. The following September, it received Party sanction as an approved mode of farming. That spelled the end of the Communes, a move which was sure to win the hearts of the farmers.

But the farmers did not get everything they wanted. Not just then anyway. This is because the conference which approved the practice of *baochan daozu* also made a point of forbidding the practice of *baochan daohu*. This was the name given to the system whereby individual households received the right to manage a farm by themselves. For the Party leadership, a *group* of households working together as an autonomous team was ok. But an *individual* household working autonomously was not ok. It was a step too far outside the bounds of Party orthodoxy. A grudging exception was made in the case of mountainous areas where the farming plots were small and far apart. In those areas, it was conceded, it did make sense for each plot to be managed by an individual household.

Although it was a minor exception, the decision to allow *baochan daohu* in the mountainous regions was to have major consequences. Because once the door to individual household-managed farms was opened even a crack, there was no closing it. Six months after conceding that *baochan daohu* could be practiced in mountainous areas, it had become acceptable also to allow it in areas of poor soil. Then more and more exceptions were claimed until the anti- *baochan daohu* faction finally gave up. By 1981 *baochan daohu* had become the dominant form of farming right throughout China. It came to be known as the Household Responsibility System.

So it was that between 1976 and 1982 rural China shifted from being organized into about 50,000 huge industrial farms to being fragmented into over one hundred million household-run farms.

Instead of a Cultural Revolution, China had just undergone an agricultural revolution.

The first impact was on the harvest itself. Between 1981 (the last year of predominantly collective farming) and 1984, the grain harvest increased by 82 million tonnes, or by 20%. Grain production per person went from 325kg in 1981 to 393kg in 1984. The hungry, discontented farmer had now become a better-fed, more-energized farmer.

The second impact was on local commerce. The town markets came alive as farmers gathered to sell their grain, and to spend their money. At the top of the list of in-demand items were fruit and vegetables, clothing and shoes, bicycles, sewing machines, radios and, for the menfolk, wristwatches. Shortages of all of these goods quickly developed. Farming equipment such as water pumps and two-wheeled tractors were also in demand, and soon were also hard to get.

The shortages spelled opportunity for the local towns. The simpler items could be manufactured right there in town. In the beginning the town councils took the lead in building the small factories that were needed. They borrowed money or raised it via taxes when they could. Then the wealthier and more entrepreneurial farmers started taking the lead, creating businesses by pooling the savings from their own farms and those of others. By 1985 these private businesses outnumbered those which were publicly-owned. Taken together, they were given a name: Town and Village Enterprises, or TVEs. A thriving rural light manufacturing sector had come into being.[24] Over time the TVEs began producing for the cities as well as the farming regions.

Such was the scale of activity that the TVEs became the engine of Chinese economic growth through the 1980s. They pulled millions of farm workers off the farms and into the towns. The available spare housing was soon taken, so construction on new apartment blocks began the length and breadth of China. Residential construction became one of China's major industries. The new apartments were not to be tiny boxes like those built in the 1950s in the big cities of Shanghai, Beijing, Wuhan and Guangzhou. Instead they were to be larger boxes – ten square metres of floorspace per person became the standard, and then that was increased to twelve.

To quantify the scale of the construction effort, consider this: in 1980 there were about 180 million people living in the villages, towns and cities of China each on average occupying a residential floorspace of about six square metres. Over the next ten years a further 100 million people moved in, for each of these an average floorspace of ten square metres was built. So through the course of the 1980s, the total stock of urban residential floorspace rose from about one billion square metres to two billion.

Alongside this residential construction came factories, power plants and all the other buildings and activities associated with urban growth. The power plants were needed because all this new development was supplied with electrical power. The factories were needed because the new apartments had to be filled with furniture and appliances. Black and white television sets were a sought-after item, although not as sought after as washing machines. Even more in demand were electric fans, sewing machines, wardrobes and lounge chairs. Naturally, new clothes were needed to fill the new wardrobes.

This spirit of consumerism extended from the towns out into the farming areas. Most farm houses had no electricity so TV sets and fans were out, but battery-powered radios were popular. Farm money was also spent on woollen blankets for the winter, pedal-driven sewing machines for making clothes, and the farm houses themselves were extended to provide a bit more living space.

This trend towards spending money should not be exaggerated. The average Chinese family maintained a frugal household, saving one third of their earnings even though they already had little to spare. These savings were then loaned to the TVEs and their city-based counterparts, which used the funds to build the power plants, factories and housing projects.

The Chinese leadership had created the environment for this wave of economic development, but they did not anticipate it and certainly did not plan it. As Deng Xiaoping said in 1987: "In the rural reform, our greatest success – and it is one we had by no means anticipated – has been the emergence of a large number of enterprises run by villages and towns. They were like a new force that just came into being spontaneously."[25]

Opening a Window to the World

At the same time as the Party leadership was reforming agriculture it was also making moves to open its economy to new ideas. These efforts were concentrated in China's south-east corner in the province of Guangdong, or Canton as it had been known in western circles for many years.

Guangdong occupied a unique position in China. It was the only province which shared a border with an advanced economy. That economy was the international port city of Hong Kong. During the Mao years, far from being seen as a good thing, this close connection to Hong Kong was viewed as a problem. This is because the people of Guangdong kept escaping over the border and setting up home in Hong Kong. It was a dangerous journey yet over the course of the 1970s at least half a million mainland Chinese had taken their chances.

Their motivation was obvious enough. Even low-paying jobs in Hong Kong paid far more than the typical wage for a Chinese urban worker. As for the difference in pay between a Hong Kong wage and that paid to a Chinese farm worker, there was no comparison. There were other attractions too. In Hong Kong there were opportunities for advancement, and there was no need to constantly proclaim allegiance to the Communist Party. In short, Hong Kong offered a much better life. No wonder so many risked everything to go there.

Hong Kong had not always been an advanced economy. Its rise had begun in the wake of the Second World War when it developed an advantage over other locations because its industrial base was not in ruins like those elsewhere. Hong Kong businesses built on this advantage to develop a thriving export trade in simple manufactures such as textiles and clothing. As time went on, they moved up to toys, and then to electronics and watches. By the 1960s the city had cemented its place as a global centre of low-cost manufacturing. By the middle of the 1970s the label Made in Hong Kong was a fixture in the retail stores of North America and western Europe.[26]

By then other industries were competing for attention in the city. Through the 1970s Asia was increasingly drawn into the global trade system, and Hong Kong was a good location for international banks and other companies to set-up their regional head offices. Thanks to its deep natural harbour, Hong Kong also became an important part of the global shipping network. Tourism grew in importance. These growing industries had the effect of pushing up average wages and land prices, thereby eroding Hong Kong's position as a low-cost manufacturer. So by the end of the 1970s, many of the factory owners were starting to look around for a new home.

It was at that time that Deng Xiaoping came to power, and the mainland Chinese attitude towards Hong Kong shifted. No longer was the city seen as a problem. Now it was seen as a place which might be able to help China develop. To explore how this might be done, two senior Red Army veterans were despatched. They were Xi Zhongxun (the father of Xi Jinping) and Yuan Geng.

At this point it will be useful to describe the geography of how Hong Kong is situated relative to China. The Pearl River is the third longest in China, and it receives the waters of many of the other rivers which run through China's southern provinces. On its way to the sea it runs through Guangdong, the capital of the province of Guangzhou, before entering the Pearl River Delta, which is great gathering point for rivers large and small as they head to the South China Sea. Hong Kong lies at the mouth of the Pearl River Delta, on its northern shore, and Macau lies opposite on the southern shore, some 25 kilometres away by ferry. Some of the land area of Hong Kong is made up of islands but most of it is on the mainland, and as such it has a land border with China. On the China side of the border lies Bao'an County.

In 1979, the largest town in Bao'an county was Shenzhen, home to about 60,000 people.[27] It sat right on the border, only about thirty kilometres from downtown Hong Kong. The main pillars of Bao'an's economy were agriculture and fishing. The fishing fleet was anchored in the sheltered inlets of Shenzhen Bay, that is when it was not out on the waters of the adjacent Pearl River Delta or the South China Sea.

Xi Zhongxun and Yuan Geng, having studied the situation, recommended that the best way to take advantage of Hong Kong was to establish business ties between companies of that city and Chinese companies. They recommended that a Hong Kong-based, Chinese government-owned shipping company called China Merchants relocate its main office to Shekou, a port area near Shenzhen. By establishing its home on the China side of the border, it was hoped that China Merchants would act as a magnet to attract business investment and skills from Hong Kong into China. The proposal quickly received approval from the Party leadership, and on January 31, 1979 the district was designated the Shekou Industrial Zone.[28]

To enhance its attractiveness to Hong Kong businesses, a range of inducements were offered. Any foreign company choosing to invest there would receive a lengthy tax holiday, and would be exempt from paying import tariffs, and also exempt from paying any export duties should they choose to manufacture goods for export. To those benefits could be added the far lower cost of land and labour when compared to nearby Hong Kong.

There was a ripple of interest from Hong Kong. It was enough to convince the Guangdong provincial officials to expand the program, so they lobbied to open up more industrial zones. They found a receptive audience, because the Communist Party Central Committee was already thinking in that direction. This was in large part because yet another senior Red Army veteran, Gu Mu, had recently returned from a fact-finding trip to Europe. There he had learned about the practice of creating industrial processing zones in which foreign companies established factories which used local labour to manufacture goods for export. Such zones were a way to attract foreign investment and expertise, and build an export-revenue earning base.

So it was that in August 1979 the whole of the Shenzhen municipal area was given the privileged status that formerly only Shekou had. At the same time, the same privileges were also granted to three other southern coastal towns. One was Zhuhai, which was next-door to Macau. The other two were Shantou, which was a day's drive up the coast, and Xiamen, which was even further north in adjoining Fujian province. They were located across the strait from Taiwan.

The idea was that these four towns were to be China's windows to the outside industrial world. Being located close to Hong Kong, Macau and Taiwan, they were in the prime position to attract foreign companies to set-up factories to produce goods for export. In this way Chinese workers would be employed in foreign-run factories and would gain first-hand exposure to modern management practices. The four towns came to be called Special Economic Zones, or SEZs. Their purpose was to get modern industry into China. It was the beginning of China's thirty-year progression from an industrial backwater to a manufacturing-for-export global colossus.

From this distance in time it is easy to imagine that the progression was a smooth one, and that the SEZ program was one long success story. That is not what happened. The reality was that the SEZ program took a long time to get off the ground. During the 1980s, it was really only in Shenzhen that much happened at all. And that was mainly because the government was prepared to pour in money. The money started to flow when the Party leadership found out that modern businesses were not going to uproot themselves and leave an international city like Hong Kong in order to set-up shop in a poverty-stricken fishing village like Shenzhen. Modern businesses needed transport and communications infrastructure, as well as access to reliable supplies of electrical power and clean water. That all cost money, and it also took time.

That Shenzhen was the first of the SEZs to get moving was entirely due to the fact that Hong Kong businesses had a big incentive to relocate. Cheap labour was the major drawcard. Shenzhen's wage rates were one tenth of what had to be paid in Hong Kong. There were other benefits too. Land costs were low, and Shenzhen was only a short drive from Hong Kong's factory districts. It was a simple matter for a firm to send its managers each day to their new factory in Shenzhen. They could return home at the end of the day. If something broke down, the spares and technical experts were only an hour away. Language and culture were no problem because many of the Hong Kong business owners had originally come from Guangdong, and many of them even had close family ties on the China side of the border.

Most of the industries which made the move were family concerns involved in labour-intensive manufactures and, as the 1980s wore on, Shenzhen became home to many small factories producing simple electrical appliances, toys and plastic goods of all kinds. Imports far outweighed exports in the early years as machinery was brought in and the local authorities imported equipment for necessary infrastructure. Exports only surpassed imports for the first in 1986. This slow progress, and the expenditure involved, raised opposition from some in the Party who thought the money would be better spent elsewhere. To paraphrase Yao Yilin, a member of the Central Committee: "Shenzhen only survives because of repeated transfusions from Beijing. It is time to pull out the syringe."[29]

But for every Yao Yilin there were others who could see the potential. Deng Xiaoping visited Shenzhen in 1984 and was impressed by the progress. So much so that later that year another fourteen coastal cities were given a status similar to Shenzhen. Second thoughts soon followed when even enthusiasts like Deng baulked at the cost of funding infrastructure development for another fourteen cities. So it was decided to concentrate on only four of them. One was Guangzhou, which was near to Shenzhen. The other three were Shanghai, Dalian and Tianjin, all major coastal cities long associated with western trading companies.

Of them all, Shenzhen remained the stand-out performer through the second half of the 1980s. By 1990, maybe half of Hong Kong's manufacturing capacity had moved there. The city ballooned in population. In 1980 it had been 60,000, by 1985 it was nearly 200,000, and by 1990 it had grown to nearly 900,000. This population influx created another attraction for Hong Kong businesspeople. The city needed ever more accommodation and infrastructure.[30] Hotels and apartment blocks were needed to serve visitors and workers, so too were power generation plants, roads and other facilities. Over forty tall office blocks, a new thing in China, were built. Much of it was funded by foreign investment, of which the majority came from Hong Kong.

So it was that in ten years Shenzhen went from being a fishing town in which most of the inhabitants lived from day-to-day to being a large and dynamic city responsible for 1% of China's 1990 GDP. That year it exported $8 billion of manufactured goods. Its factories were responsible for 13% of China's foreign trade.[31]

This was not due to an inspired feat of Communist Party policy-making. Instead it was due to the simple fact that the owners of Hong Kong's world-class manufacturing industry were prepared to move their factories thirty kilometres up the road because the economics made sense and the Chinese government was prepared to spend whatever it took to get them there.

There is another way of looking at it. The Shenzhen success showed how pragmatic was the Chinese leadership, how quickly Chinese workers could adapt and how rapidly the urban environment could be transformed. It probably gave confidence to the Central Committee when in the mid-1980s they took on the next task: shifting China's many large city-based industrial businesses onto a more dynamic and competitive footing.

The Urban Revolution is Not So Successful

When the reform era began, China's cities were home to about one in five Chinese. There was a policy of segregation in place right across the country. It was called *hukou,* or the household registration system. Under this policy, a person was designated as an urban or a rural resident, and further designated as a resident of a particular city or a particular agricultural region. *Hukou* required that a person born in Shanghai must be educated, live and work, and grow old in Shanghai. Likewise, a person born in a particular agricultural region must spend their lives in that region.

This policy meant that the urban population of China had stayed at about 20% of the total population for the past twenty years. The cities had grown alongside, but separate from, the farming regions. Into the cities came agricultural goods, coal and minerals. Out from the cities went manufactured goods and electrical power.

Nearly all city dwellers of working age were employed in either a government department, the military or a large business. These businesses could be involved either in manufacturing, transport, power generation, construction, retail or some other field. They have become known as State-Owned Enterprises, or SOEs.

All of the SOEs were large, highly structured and hierarchical. They were also responsible for the social well-being of their workers and their families. They owned the apartment blocks where their workers and their families lived, they provided them education, childcare and healthcare facilities, and even ran the stores at which they shopped.

In the Mao era, the managers of the SOEs were governed by the Five Year Plan. The Plan told them how many items to make, and it provided them with the people and material which were deemed necessary to achieve that outcome. The Five Year Plan was nothing less than a book which detailed the allocation of all the human and material resources within China's industrial economy. There was no value in attempting to buck or even to question the Plan. It was necessary simply to accept it and try to work the system so that the promised manpower and materials were actually delivered.

It led to a culture of management by shrugging things off.[32] This became especially true during the Cultural Revolution when a manager was judged by his or her ability to demonstrate unswerving adherence to the Party line. The workers were judged in a similar way: their principal task was to maintain appearances in the political indoctrination sessions. For manager and worker alike, putting in effort at work came a distant second. There was no reward for such effort, they were paid their small salary regardless. As Deng Xiaoping put it in a speech to a Party Congress in 1978: "[During the Cultural Revolution] no distinction was made between those who worked well and those who didn't. In some cases, people who worked well were attacked while those who did nothing or just played it safe weathered every storm. Under those unwritten laws, people were naturally reluctant to use their brains."[33]

Deng had long considered it his job to change this. As far back as 1975, when the Cultural Revolution was still dominating the political scene, he told the audience of senior managers at a conference on iron and steel manufacture: "The main cause of our sluggish iron and steel production is the leadership, which is weak, lazy and lax." To be fair, a weak and lax leadership style would probably have been helpful to survival during the worst years of the Cultural Revolution. But now that that storm had passed, Deng wanted senior managers to regain their courage. He went on to say: "How can an individual be allowed to be casually absent from work whenever he feels like it? If a man doesn't come to work, cross his name off the payroll. If he refuses to work, tell him to leave!"

Deng's point was clear enough: China had a very poorly managed industrial base, where production targets fell short and waste went unchecked. By the time he took the helm in 1978, the scope for improvement in the urban factory system was even greater than it was on the farm.

The task of fixing the problem was assigned to Zhao Ziyang. He started by trying out a system whereby managers would be rewarded for improving profits. After all it had worked very well in agriculture. His scheme was even called the Contract Responsibility System,[34] in a direct imitation of the Household Responsibility System.

The problem was that improving performance in manufacturing was not quite as straightforward as it was on the farm. This was because the factory managers, unlike the farmers, had very little control over their factories. They could not hire or fire because workers had lifetime employment, they could not increase their output because they had little ability to increase purchases of supplies, nor could they earn more revenue by raising the quality of their products because the selling price was fixed.

After a few years of trying out the Contract Responsibility System it had become clear that more far-reaching reforms were needed if the factory productivity was to improve. To be more specific about it, the system of fixed outputs and fixed prices, in place since the early 1950s and much-loved by the Communist Party rank and file, had to be replaced by the free market, or at least a free-er market. And for that happen, the system of fixed prices had to be abandoned, or at least partly abandoned. Politically, that was no easy thing to do.

The fixed price system was one of the more popular legacies of the Mao years. In many cases, prices had been set in the 1950s and altered only a little since. People had become accustomed to the security that these unchanging prices gave them. The reformers knew that price reform had to be approached with caution.

The first "baby step" was taken in 1984, and impacted only a small set of items. It went well enough for a second much larger step to be authorised by the Central Committee, and it went ahead in 1987. Effectively this step created a price system which was supposed to be a happy halfway point between the fixed price system and the free market. Unfortunately, it turned out to be the worst of both worlds.

To explain this, Zhao's new halfway system decreed that China's state-owned factories were required to produce for two markets. Each factory was required to produce a certain quantity of goods in order to supply their existing state-owned enterprise customers. Those goods were to be supplied at the existing fixed prices. Once those goods were supplied, any excess production could then be sold on the open market, at prices determined by the market. It was called the dual price system.[35]

The market prices were always going to be higher than the fixed prices. And the main market for the excess factory production was out in the countryside. Given this, the dual price system could be described in another way: there was to be a fixed price for city-based customers, and then there was to be a much-higher price for customers living in the towns and villages outside the cities.

The dual price system really should have worked quite well. After all, in China's farming regions in the second half of the 1980s there was huge demand for housing and household goods of all kinds. Factory managers in Beijing, Shanghai or Wuhan now had official permission, and encouragement, to expand their factories and sell the extra output in the towns and villages of the surrounding provinces. They would gain a good bonus for doing so. Deng and his colleagues hoped, and no doubt expected, that this would result in an urban economic transformation of the kind seen in the farming regions.

But it did not quite work out that way. This because the hoped-for economic transformation had to happen within the state-owned enterprises and they were bloated bureaucracies staffed with apathetic workers who knew their jobs to be untouchable. The factory managers had not the skills to drive expansion plans through this organisational quicksand, nor had they the skills to motivate their workforce to achieve greater things. Their skills were much more suited to a different pursuit: taking advantage of any weaknesses in the system. And with Zhao's new halfway pricing system, there was plenty of opportunity to do exactly that.

To illustrate this, take the case of a factory manager who was contracted to supply a truckload of winter clothing to the employees of a large urban hospital. Given that the hospital was part of the fixed price system, the factory manager knew that only the fixed price could be charged. That manager also knew, however, that a much higher price could be obtained if, by some mistake, the truckload of clothing was sent into the countryside, where the clothing would be sold to villagers. So mistakes would happen. Regularly. The countryfolk ended-up satisfied. So did the factory manager because he or she usually managed to pocket much of the windfall. But the hospital employees were not satisfied. They missed out on their new winter clothing.

In short, Zhao's halfway price system allowed corruption to flourish. It also allowed inflation to start creeping in. It began in the countryside and inevitably made its way into the cities. When compared to the bouts of inflation seen in 1970s Latin America and elsewhere, China's inflation during the late 1980s was mild. It never exceeded 30% per year and was unremarkable given the country's galloping economy. But it was being imposed on a populace who, for 25 years, had lived in an economy where prices hardly changed at all. They had long ago worked out their household budget and knew what they could afford to buy, and what they could put away for a rainy day. Now their careful planning was out the window. It caused anger and fear of the future.

Deng Xiaoping and his colleagues were aware of the anger stirred up by the corruption and inflation. In an attempt to solve both of them, Deng decided to take the bull by the horns. Ever the advocate of bold action he pushed a hesitant Zhao Ziyang to declare a policy of full and sudden price liberalization. The idea was that it would get rid of corruption, and it would also get rid of persistent inflation. Yes, it would probably result in an initial sharp bout of inflation. But that was preferable to the ongoing pain of continuing steady inflation.

Zhao was not convinced but Deng Xiaoping was not man to be defied. The result was that, in June 1988, Zhao duly announced that China's price system was to be fully liberalised.[36] It came as a shock to a public already nervous about price rises. Panic buying broke out in several cities, causing inflation to worsen. The backlash was so fierce that the policy was withdrawn, but not before a lot of damage had been done to public trust in the reform process. So, as 1988 came to a close, the stark reality had to be faced. Nearly ten years of reform efforts had had almost no impact on the urban factory system. Worse still, a mood of bitter discontent was building in the cities.

Tiananmen Square

There is a political bargain in China which has been in place since the Communists came to power. This bargain is that the Party promises to deliver economic progress and in return it expects to retain all political power. In the Mao years only lip service was paid to economic progress. This neglect of the Party's side of the bargain was one reason why the successors to Mao moved so rapidly with their reforms. They were fearful that the people would rise up when they knew that China's hardest man, Chairman Mao, was gone.

The two-way nature of the bargain has been taken very seriously ever since. The Party has been much more committed to economic progress and improving the living standards of the people. In return, it has continued to demand that the people be fully accepting of the Party's retention of all political power. The bargain has worked well. So well in fact that China's remarkable economic transformation has unfolded with only one serious clash between the Party and the people.

That clash is known in China as the June 4 Incident.[37] Outside China it is known as the Tiananmen Square massacre. At its heart it was a challenge to the legitimacy of the Communist Party's right to govern as it sees fit. These are not issues that the Party wants discussed, so, even now, thirty years later, public discussion of the June 4 Incident is forbidden in China.

The first step on the road to the June 4 Incident was taken in December 1986 when students held protests on a dozen university campuses across China. They were calling for something to be done to curb the high-level corruption and needless abuses of power which had become increasingly public. The most visible example of this was the behaviour of the children of high-ranking Party officials. These 20 and 30 year olds, known as the princelings, thumbed their noses at the common people by driving around the cities in their luxury cars, flaunting their wealth. It did not go down well with the students.

The student protests were a new thing in China. In the Mao years, they would not have dared. But with the liberalisation of the economy, students had become emboldened. Not willing to tolerate such a challenge, Deng Xiaoping ordered his deputy, Hu Yaobang, to close them down. Hu then did something which was quite radical for a senior Communist Party member: he refused to do it.[38] It is not clear why. No doubt he had sympathy for the aims of the protesters. Still, his job as Deng's political fixer was to manage such issues.

Whatever his reason, Hu's days were numbered after that. The conservatives had never much liked him and this was their chance. A month after he had defied his boss, he was forced to resign. If they had been strong enough, the conservatives would also have pushed out Zhao Ziyang. They liked him even less. But Zhao had gained a lot of the credit for the progress of the economy and he was a harder target. With Hu gone, the campuses were restored to order, and the students went back to class.

The whole incident was fairly a minor disturbance as far as the public went. But it had exposed the deep divisions within the Party caused by the pace of the economic reforms. Seeing the need to calm things down, Deng Xiaoping seized on Hu's resignation as a chance to do some reorganisation. He appointed Zhao Ziyang as Hu's replacement. This looked like a promotion but in reality Zhao was being kicked upstairs. Deng's main intention was to instal a conservative to the role of chief economic reformer. Accordingly, he appointed Li Peng, a leading conservative, to the job.

Li, like all of the senior Chinese political leaders, was supportive of the overall aims of the reform process. He had, for example, in a speech at one the Party's national conferences, called for closer links to western economies and a speeding-up of development in the SEZs. But, like all of the conservatives, he thought that more caution should be exercised in introducing the changes. For this reason, he was determined to slow down the overall pace of economic reform. His appointment by Deng was a public acknowledgement that the reform process was going too fast.

Zhao was not a man to be easily kicked upstairs. He had lost direct oversight of the economic reform process, so he set about getting it back. This he did by developing an extension of socialist economic theory. China, according to this theory, was in the first stage of its transition to socialism, and socialist theory (according to Zhao) decreed that during this first stage it was necessary to use market-oriented policies. Whatever the merits of this argument, the Party found it convincing and over the next year or so Zhao regained his economic leadership. With Zhao back in the driver's seat, 1988 was a year of bold reform announcements. There was to be a new law which would allow land leases to be bought and sold. There was to be a full opening of the economy to foreign investment. And, at Deng's insistence, there was to be a full liberalisation of prices.

The price liberalisation (as already described) was an immediate disaster and it was officially withdrawn about a week later. Although it was Deng's policy, he was untouchable, so Zhao was painted as its architect and for the second time was pushed away from the controls of economic policy. Li Peng, now back at the controls, laid down the law. He decreed that there would be a two-year freeze on reforms while the country digested the reforms already implemented. China's economic reform process had, in effect, been brought to a stop.

About a year into this reform-halt, Hu Yaobang died. He was seen by the students as a kindred spirit and an honest man prepared to take a stand against official corruption. He had, the students believed, been sacked for defending the rights of the Chinese people. So the evening before his State funeral a crowd of 100,000 gathered in Tiananmen Square to pay their respects. The Party leadership were surprised by the number and passion of those assembled.

The huge crowd did not disperse after the funeral. Instead, here and there protests started up. It was a volatile situation which needed deft handling. And that is exactly what did not happen. In a masterstroke of bad timing, the day after Hu's state funeral Zhao Ziyang departed for an official visit to North Korea. His departure removed the one man who may have been able to defuse the situation. With him gone, the handling of the protesters was left to Deng Xiaoping and Li Peng, both of whom had little tolerance for student protests. They wrote an editorial in a leading newspaper which accused the protesters of being in sympathy with those who would "plunge the country into chaos and sabotage". It was intended to frighten the students. It succeeded only in angering them. The situation deteriorated from there.

Throughout May the crowd in the Square grew and became more demanding. They wanted faster reform of the urban factories, a move towards democracy and a tougher crackdown on corruption. Above all, they wanted the editorial retracted. Hunger strikes began on May 13 and these attracted so much public sympathy that on May 17 one million people gathered to show their support. To add to that, the unrest was spreading to other Chinese cities. Confronted by a rapidly spreading crisis, the regional Party officials stood by, unsure of what to do.

In contrast, the central Party leadership was increasingly sure of what to do, and it involved forcibly clearing the Square. Sensing danger, on May 19 Zhao Ziyang made a pre-dawn speech to the protesters. Using a bullhorn and standing in the middle of a crowd, he apologised for the editorial, promised further dialogue and pleaded with the students to stop the hunger strikes. He no doubt thought he was doing the best thing in the circumstances. But his Party colleagues did not think so. It was his last ever public appearance.

The next day, martial law was declared in Beijing. Two weeks later, on June 4, the army cleared the Square, killing at least 200 people. That is the Communist Party's body count. A report the day after the massacre by the British Ambassador to China put the number killed at 10,000.[39] A China-wide crackdown followed, aimed at crushing any hint of public sympathy for the protesters.

The June 4 Incident shocked China. It also led to upheaval in the upper echelons of the Communist Party. Zhao Ziyang was stripped of his positions and placed under house arrest, where he would stay until his death fifteen years later.[40] Deng Xiaoping was pushed aside. The conservatives said that the whole fiasco was the result of too much reform, too fast. Not content with stopping the reform process, they now threatened to reverse it.

If the reforms had been reversed, it may well have been the end of China's economic transformation before it really began. But threats of reversal were as far as the conservatives went. The reformers, led by Deng Xiaoping, re-grouped and pushed back. They blocked the appointment of a conservative to replace Zhao Zhiyang. Instead a compromise candidate was chosen. This was Jiang Zemin, mayor of Shanghai. Jiang had managed the June 4 crisis well, keeping order in Shanghai without using heavy-handed tactics. He was a member of neither the conservative nor the reform factions, and he had never served in the army. So he had no power base to lean on. His elevation was mainly due to his being acceptable to both sides.

Jiang's appointment set the tone of the next few years. In other words, there was a stalemate. The reforms already achieved stayed in effect, but little more was done. China sat on the fence, waiting for someone to make a move.

Chapter 3

THE 1990s

The Southern Tour

In the year which followed the June 4 Incident, China's economic growth rate fell back to 4%. That was the worst economic performance in many years and followed nearly a decade of +10% growth rate. The slowdown was a deliberate policy. Li Peng's priority was to stop the inflation which was causing so much concern among the urban population. To achieve it, he reined in spending by the state-owned enterprises, and he cancelled many of the infrastructure projects which had been planned for next few years.[41]

It worked and inflation was declared dead in early 1990. With this having been achieved, there was something of a thaw in economic policy. The brakes were partially released from the reform agenda. Li Peng approved the creation of the Pudong SEZ in Shanghai, throwing open the door to China's largest city. Work resumed on the stalled infrastructure projects, and the state-owned enterprises were permitted once more to invest. Private business owners, sensing that things were returning to normal, also started spending once more. So too did the households across China. Even foreign investors began to return with their chequebooks. The economic growth rate picked up a bit.

But it was a meek recovery and for that reason, by 1991, the mood of the Party was turning back in favour of the reformers. Voices were once again being raised to make the case for economic reform. The loudest and most authoritative of them was, as always, that of Deng Xiaoping. He made speeches and spoke at Party meetings throughout the year. But even he could not get the reform process moving again. So at the end of 1991, he resolved to take matters into his own hands. He decided to embark on his now-famous speaking tour.

The Southern Tour, as it has come to be known, began in Wuhan, on 18 January 1992. It passed through three cities in Guangdong - Shenzhen, Zhuhai and Guangzhou - before turning north to Shanghai and Nanjing and finishing in the city of Bengbu in Anhui Province, on 21 February. Deng chose each of these cities because they had all made considerable economic progress through the 1980s. His purpose was to highlight what could be achieved when economic reforms were boldly followed.

In each of the cities he visited, Deng met with influential figures and gave after-dinner speeches. One of these speeches – the one for which the Southern Tour is most remembered – was delivered in Shenzhen. He began with: "During my trip here, I have found that the rapid growth in the Shenzhen and Zhuhai Special Economic Zones and some other areas has exceeded my expectations."[43]

But he was not there to pat people on the back: "At first, people were not enthusiastic about rural reform, and many waited to see how it would work.… It was my idea to discourage contention, so as to have more time for action. Once disputes begin, they complicate matters and waste a lot of time. As a result, nothing is accomplished. Don't argue; try bold experiments and blaze new trails. That's the way it was with rural reform, and that's the way it should be with urban reform."

Deng went on to say: "It is crucial to expand the economy. The economies of some of our neighbouring countries and regions are growing faster than ours. If our economy stagnates or develops only slowly, the people will make comparisons and ask why. Therefore, those areas that are in a position to develop should not be obstructed. Where local conditions permit, development should proceed as fast as possible. There is nothing to worry about so long as we stress efficiency and quality and develop an export-oriented economy. Slow growth equals stagnation and even retrogression. We must grasp opportunities; the present offers an excellent one. The only thing I worry about is that we may lose opportunities. If we don't seize them, they will slip through our fingers as time speeds by."

It was a call to action. Deng was saying to the gathered businesspeople and officials that it was safe now to start once more pushing hard on building the economy. And they should waste no time in going about it otherwise other countries – Malaysia, South Korea and Thailand for example – would be the winners and China would be the loser.

The Southern Tour might have fallen flat, stirring up some conversation but not achieving anything. But Deng had been involved in politics long enough to know how to push an agenda. His speech was published in a widely-read newspaper, letting the Chinese public know that powerful figures were pushing for a return to rapid economic growth. And his words emboldened the many in government who wanted to preside once again over a galloping economy. Most importantly, Deng used the Southern Tour to prove to the hesitant Jiang Zemin that there was plenty of support for a return to rapid reforms. His case was strengthened by the conclusion of a recently-published report into the collapse of the Soviet Union, which had occurred just a few years before. The report blamed, among other things, a dogmatic and inflexible Soviet leadership which had failed to move with the times.

Deng's arguments were not lost on Jiang. He had been a compromise candidate for a reason: he had a good sense of which way the wind was blowing. And the wind was now blowing in favour of re-energising the reform process. Accordingly, later that year, at the 14th National Conference of the Chinese Communist Party, Jiang showed that he was fully on-board with faster reforms when he declared that China was henceforth to be a "socialist market economy".[44] The important word was "market". It meant that China was no longer to be a planned economy, and was instead to be a market economy. The reform process was back on the front burner.

Deng Xiaoping would not stay as the power behind the throne for very much longer. He was 88 and his health was failing. In one of his last important moves before he retired permanently from the national stage, he used his influence to ensure that Zhu Rongji was elected to the Politburo Standing Committee, China's top decision-making body. Zhu, according to Deng, "has his own views, dares to make decisions and understands economics." To make sure no-one missed his point: "he is the only one who understands economics." With Jiang Zemin and Zhu Rongji ranged against him, Li Peng was outgunned. From 1993, the reformers were back in control.

Foreign Investment

It did not take very long for news of the Southern Tour to reach the outside world. By April 1992, three months after Deng's Shenzhen speech, it was clear that foreign investors had revised their view of China. Money was starting to pour in. To illustrate this in numbers: in 1991 total foreign investment in China came to just under $4 billion. That was about the same as the level in 1988, meaning that foreign investment had been flat for four years. In 1992, it rose sharply, reaching $10 million. Then in 1993 it jumped to nearly $30 billion. The next year it was $34 billion and in 1995 it climbed even further, reaching nearly $40 billion. It was a tenfold increase in just four years. Either Deng Xiaoping was the most convincing after-dinner speaker in history, or something else was driving this.

To better understand the drivers, a good place to start is by looking at where the money came from. As far as official figures went, nearly two thirds of it came from Hong Kong. This is not surprising given that Hong Kong had been the leading investor right through the 1980s. But the official figures concealed an important new trend.

Much of the money being invested by Hong Kong businesses was only being channelled through that city. It was originating in Taiwan.

The economic rise of Taiwan needs some explanation.[45] Up until the end of the Second World War, Taiwan had for fifty years been a colony of Japan. With the defeat of the Japanese in 1945, Chiang Kai-Shek and his Chinese Nationalist Party claimed it for China. When the Communists defeated the Nationalists, Chiang Kai-Shek set sail with his army for Taiwan, arriving with their families and accompanied by refugees.

Before long Chiang Kai-Shek was leading the island's government. In contrast to his predatory behaviour when in power in China, in Taiwan he set about building a strong economy and a democratic government. The economic development path he took initially mirrored what was happening in mainland China. Just as on the mainland, Chiang's first step was land reform in favour of the small farmers. When land reform was completed, in 1952 came the first Four Year Plan (he chose four years, not five, so as not to be accused of copying the Communists). Instead of focussing on heavy industry, however, Chiang Kai-Shek's Plan charted a path for the development of light manufacturing. So successful was it that by the early 1970s the country had become an important global exporter of processed food and manufactured consumer goods. The biggest advantage Taiwan had was its low labour cost. This was helped by the modernisation of its farms, a development which created plenty of surplus farm labourers, who then moved to the factories.

The next stage of the country's development began in the early 1960s when firms in Japan, under pressure from rising wages in their own country, began to outsource their manufacturing operations to Taiwan. Why Taiwan and not one of the several South East Asian nations which at the time were beginning to establish a manufacturing base? Taiwan had three advantages. It was geographically closer to Japan, it was familiar terrain for the Japanese having been a long-time colony until twenty years ago, and, most importantly, Japan's trading companies still maintained a strong presence in Taiwan. So the lion's share of the Japanese manufacturing which moved offshore in the 1960s and 70s found a home in Taiwan.

Japanese textiles, processed food and chemicals companies were first in. Then it was the turn of the electrical and electronics companies. By the mid-1960s Toshiba, Sanyo, Panasonic and Hitachi had set up manufacturing operations. They were followed by their US competitors. Two of the largest – IBM and RCA – were running factories in Taiwan by 1970.

Things grew from there.[46] Taiwanese manufacturing increased in size and scope through the 1970s and 80s until the country was one of the major global locations for the production of consumer electronics and many other household goods. But time was running out for its low cost manufacturing model. Firstly, wages were increasing as the supply of surplus farm workers began dry up. Secondly, Taiwan got caught up in the dispute between the US and Japan over what the US saw as the unfair trade advantage Japan was getting by keeping its currency artificially weak versus the US dollar. The dispute was resolved by the Plaza Accord of 1985, with the result that the Taiwanese dollar rose about 30% versus the US dollar. Taiwan's exports were now much more expensive.

The wage rises coupled with the currency shifts meant that by the early 1990s Taiwanese manufacturers were coming under a lot of pressure. So when, during his Southern Tour of 1992, Deng Xiaoping proclaimed that China was once again open for business, Taiwanese businesses took notice. They shared the language and culture, and many of them had family ties in the mainland coastal cities. For them, mainland China was a very acceptable manufacturing location. Hong Kong property developers, seeing the new wave of optimism generated by the Southern Tour, felt the same way.

So in 1992, these two investor groups were primed and ready to move their money and assets into China. Compared to the first wave of foreign investment which had come from Hong Kong family-owned manufacturers and was concentrated in Shenzhen, this second wave was much larger. From 1992, Taiwanese and Hong

Kong businesspeople were arriving in China looking for suitable sites for their factories and hotels.[47]

With all these foreigners knocking on the door holding bags of money, the municipal governments in the coastal cities went into overdrive. They knew how to win over investors, and were not shy of being aggressive to do it. They had been developing and honing those skills since the early 1980s. That was when Deng and his allies had devised a new evaluation process for a Party member's advancement through the ranks. The new process made clear that advancement would be solely dependent on that Party member securing new business investment and economic growth for his or her municipal area.

The change had been made because Deng knew that only a drastic measure could shake the city officials out of thirty years of Maoist behaviour. He knew he had to push them into removing the obstacles confronting China's new class of private investors wanting to invest their own money in a business. In the early days there were plenty of such obstacles. They included jealous managers in state-owned enterprises who were protecting their turf, lack of facilities to support new factories, a lack of skilled and available workers, red tape and high local taxes and charges. Often, even usually, the private business only succeeded because they had the backing and active support of the mayor or someone else in the city government.

The measure had worked. By the 1990s, the city governments in China had experience and real skills in attracting new factories and other investment for their cities. It could even be said that the government of every Chinese city was now primarily focussed on attracting investors and solving problems for them. Everyone at every level in the bureaucracy had their targets for how much investment they had to attract. There were promotions and bonuses for those who brought in new projects. Sometimes getting the signature on the deal was easy enough, but on many other occasions a bidding war for the investment broke out between rival cities. Special tax breaks, cheap land, project specific infrastructure and all sorts of other inducements were offered. It was a fight to the finish.

Being courted in this way, tens of thousands of foreign factories set-up in China's coastal cities during the 1990s. Mostly they were small affairs, costing between $2 and $10 million to build and equip. In the first few years the majority of businesses were geared to the production of low-value goods such as textiles, clothing, footwear, and a whole range of plastic items. Later on came white goods and electronics manufacture. Huge industrial estates were developed to accommodate all this new manufacturing capacity. These estates required infrastructure including cleared and levelled land, power and water supply, transport and communication links and services such as waste removal. Then there was accommodation for the workers. Often the foreign companies themselves built dormitories, and where that was not sufficient, apartment blocks were constructed by local developers. It was urban development on the fast track.[48]

So it was that over the course of the 1990s China became a centre of global manufacturing. Its exports increased fourfold over the decade, making it the world's fifth largest trading nation, up from fifteenth in 1990. Foreign companies with manufacturing-for-export factories accounted for half of the exports. Much of this was owed to the tidal wave of investment from Taiwanese manufacturers, and a second wave of investment from Hong Kong. The Chinese government had not performed any miracles in attracting them. They had simply been in the right place at the right time with an open door. In the space of 20 years, two globally important centres of export manufacturing - Taiwan and Hong Kong - had, in effect, shifted to China.

Migration to the Cities

The flood of foreign investment was a big driver of the growth of the Chinese economy during the 1990s. The coastal cities attracted almost all of it. Those cities were, after all, the closest to Taiwan and Hong Kong, and it was far easier doing business there than in the interior. This concentration of foreign investment meant that the coastal cities developed their infrastructure much more quickly than did those in the interior and they became much more adept at the competitive business of attracting new investment. All of which meant that they were more attractive locations for the home-grown Chinese companies looking to expand and push into the cities.[49]

All of which meant that, during the 1990s, the coastal cities were the main centres of growth in the factory system in China. Workers were needed and it did not take long for the local supply of them to be exhausted. The city governments were not going to allow a shortage of labour slow things down. So they encouraged the local farmers to move to the city. When the supply of local farmers ran out, they encouraged farmers from further away. When that was not enough, they beckoned to farmers from the next province. The result was a constant stream of new workers entering the cities, which inevitably created a sharp increase in their population.

This increase in the population of the country's major cities was a new and important development in the modern history of China. It also gave rise to an entirely new phenomenon in Communist China: the migrant worker. To appreciate the significance of it all, some background is needed.

From its earliest years, the Chinese Communist government was concerned to control the population of the cities. Having made the decision to prioritise a program of heavy industrial development, the Party leadership also made the decision to fund the program by requisitioning the surplus grain from the farming regions. Knowing that this would make the cities look like very desirable places to live, they put in place formal restrictions on how and when people could move from farm to city.

In 1958, as part of the Great Leap Forward, this policy was formalised into the *hukou* system.[50] The system broke down during the chaotic years of the Great Leap Forward but in the years which followed it was restored. Through the rest of the Mao era it was tightly managed. So much so that, when Deng Xiaoping came to power in 1978, only 18% of the population lived in the cities. That percentage had remained unchanged since 1962.

This separation of city and country continued through the 1980s but the urbanisation rate began to rise. It climbed from 19% to 26% of the Chinese population over the course of the decade. To put that in terms of actual people: in 1980 there were 190 million Chinese living in designated urban areas. In 1990 this figure was 300 million. Those statistics would suggest a shift of 110 million people from country to city, but in fact only about 20 million people had moved from the farm to an actual city. The rest had not moved to an actual city at all, rather they had only shifted a few kilometres from their farm to a nearby village, or they had shifted a bit further and settled in a regional town.

The confusion was caused by the definition of what an urban area was. It had been decided back in the 1960s that an urban area was any municipality with a population above 3,000 people. So while the urbanisation rate climbed in the 1980s, that was because many people moved off the land and found jobs in small workshops and factories in the local villages and towns. For the most part, those people did not move very far at all, staying within their *hukou* district. A good many of the new urban dwellers did not actually move at all. They stayed where they were and found themselves reclassified as urban dwellers because their village of, say, 2,000 had increased in population to over 3,000. So during the 1980s, the *hukou* system stayed intact and the population of the cities did not increase much. The engine of economic growth was in the countryside.

That all changed in the 1990s. The engine of economic growth was now located in the coastal cities and as a result their population grew very rapidly. To put some figures around it: the urban population of China went from 26% in 1990 to 40% in 2000. The total urban population rose from 300 million to 470 million, and the bulk of those 170 million new urban residents were farm and village workers who had moved to the coastal cities.[51]

The Pearl River Delta saw the largest increases.[52] It had been the biggest beneficiary from foreign investment and was certainly the centre of China's assembly-for-export factories. It was bristling with office buildings and apartment blocks. Industrial parks stretched for miles in every direction. The horizon was punctuated by power stations pluming their smoke into the sky. The once small regional cities had blossomed into major ones. Dongguan, situated mid-way between Shenzhen and Guangzhou, went from having a population of half a million in 1990 to a population of nearly four million in 2000. Foshan, sitting just outside Guangzhou, went from nearly one million to four million. Shenzhen, unsurprisingly, was the poster-city for urban population growth. It went from being home to one million people to being home to more than six million. In total, the city-based population of the Pearl River Delta grew from seven to twenty six million over the decade.

Similar population rises, if not on quite the same scale, happened all along the coast. The two trading cities of Fujian province – Xiamen and Fuzhou – had a combined population of just over one million in 1990. This had risen to nearly four million ten years later. Shanghai, China's largest city, had a population of nearly eight million in 1990. This had risen to over fourteen million by the end of the decade. Beijing saw a similar rise, finishing the decade with a population of ten million.

Those who made the move were known as migrant workers. The term was intended to underscore the lack of permanence in their position. The city authorities turned a blind eye to the fact that they were in the city illegally. They knew that without the workers their efforts to attract investment would be wasted. The workers were needed, it did not matter where they came from.

In fact, for many of the new factories the migrant workers were essential. This is because they were willing to work for low wages and the company employing them was not obliged to pay them any welfare benefits. That made them very cheap labour. In contrast, those workers with an urban *hukou* expected higher wages and were entitled to considerable welfare benefits. The foreign investors and private company owners avoided the urban *hukou* workers where they could. Their business model relied on keeping costs down. The migrant workers were in demand.

It was for this reason that through the 1990s a constant stream of single men, single women and young families left the rural areas and made their way to the cities. The city authorities welcomed them as long as they found work. Those that arrived and did not find work tended not to stay to long. There was no welfare safety net for them, and being illegal residents they were harassed and eventually chased out. But the great majority of them did find work.

It was this willing, cheap and 100 million strong labour force which transformed the Chinese cities during the 1990s. One of their most important impacts was unintended: they provided a formidable weapon for the reformers when they decided once more to take on the toughest task of all – the reform of the state-owned enterprises.

Reforming the State-Owned Enterprise

At the start of the 1990s, with the exception of foreign-owned businesses, all of the large industrial and commercial concerns in China were owned and operated by either the central government in Beijing, the provincial government or by the city-level municipal government. In 1990 there were at least 100,000 of these state-owned enterprises. Collectively, they controlled a very large part of the national economy including all heavy industry, large-scale construction, power generation, transport, communications, petroleum, mining and smelting and even most of the large urban retail outlets. Most of city-based light manufacturing was also under their control.

About seven in ten city workers had a job in one of them. This meant that in total they employed about 140 million people. When all the dependents of those employees were added, there were more than 300 million Chinese who relied on the companies for their accommodation, education, health care and retirement benefits. This is because they were still operating under the Mao era model whereby the state took on the responsibility for providing everything that the workers and their families needed.

A job in one of these state-owned companies was a job for life. It was known as the "iron rice bowl" because the state guaranteed that the worker's supply of food, signified by the rice bowl, could not be broken.[53] The state-owned enterprises were nominally run as profit-making businesses, but in reality profits came second. Their top priority was keeping their employees in a job and supporting their families. Unsurprisingly, given these requirements, they were not very dynamic organisations.

In an attempt to improve their competitive performance, over the second half of the 1980s the three levels of government had loaned them a good deal of money. The money was used to fund purchases of additional equipment, factory upgrades, the construction of new facilities and so on. It did not have the desired effect. By the early 1990s, at least half, and probably closer to two thirds, of the state-owned companies were losing money. When all the subsidies and waived debts were included, the central government had in 1994 spent half of its annual budget in propping them up. As a result, it was facing a financial crisis of its own.

It was not the economy which was making the state-owned businesses struggle. Right alongside them was a vibrant private sector which was making good money, and doing so in part by taking market share from the state-owned companies. The situation was untenable. Everyone knew that the state-owned businesses needed reform. Yet there was a reluctance to tackle it. Any serious reform was going to face plenty of opposition from politically-connected executives, and from the workers themselves. The whole idea of reform brought with it the possibility of worker lay-offs. The cities were already facing a challenge to absorb all the migrant workers. They did not need the challenge of absorbing tens of millions more laid-off and angry urban workers. The Tiananmen Square demonstrations had been triggered by far less.

Yet the reform had to be done. The task was eventually given to Zhu Rong-Ji.[54] He was at the time a Vice Premier of China, reporting to the Premier, Li Peng. As Vice Premier his role was to take on thorny economic issues, and they did not come much thornier than this.

Zhu's career is worth recounting briefly, because he ranks higher even than Zhao Ziyang in his contribution to China's forty-year economic miracle. During his early career he had suffered the usual ups and downs. Appointed to an important position at a young age, he had in 1957 made the mistake of saying aloud that one of Chairman Mao's policies was irrational (which it no doubt was). For that he had been expelled from the Communist Party. About a year later his wealthy family's house was destroyed by a mob, although that was probably unrelated to his indiscretion about Mao.

After a period of re-education he was permitted to re-join the Party, given a job as an engineer in the Ministry of Petroleum and then purged again during the Cultural Revolution. This time he was sent to work as a farm labourer for six years. When Mao died, Zhu was brought back to the Ministry of Petroleum. He was clearly a capable operator because by 1983 he had been appointed to the position of Vice Minister of the State Economic Commission.

His big step upward came in 1987 when he was appointed mayor of Shanghai, China's largest and wealthiest city. He removed many of the obstacles to the city's development, and in the process took a tough stance on corruption. The result was that, during his tenure, Shanghai went from being in the slow lane of economic development to surpassing Shenzhen as the most dynamic city in China. His biggest achievement while in this position was the development of the Pudong district.

The history of the Pudong development, given its significance in China's economic rise, also deserves a brief recounting. The Huangpu is a short river which flows from south to north through the centre of Shanghai. The district on its west bank is called Puxi, and the district on its east bank, Pudong. Puxi had long been considered the better side of the river, and even up until the late 1980s was where all the factories and commercial buildings were located. The Pudong district was avoided, and for the most part remained as agricultural land. It was a large area, covering over one thousand square kilometres.[55]

Which meant that there was one thousand square kilometres of farmland sitting across the river from the centre of China's biggest city. It had easy access to the Yangtze river, easy access to the country's largest port and easy access to all the commercial acumen and business contacts the nation could offer. Could there be a more perfect location for foreign businesses looking to set up in China? In March 1990, Zhu Rong-Ji submitted a proposal for opening up and developing Pudong, and it was accepted by Li Peng. The district was granted the status of a Special Economic Zone and from that point it became the most sought-after location in the country. Every significant corporation in the world wanted an office and factory in Pudong. With all the construction that followed, Shanghai's economy entered a boom which is still going on. It was said at one time that one quarter of all the world's cranes were operating in Shanghai. Whilst that was an exaggeration, it painted the picture of the scale of construction which Pudong attracted.

Deng Xiaoping was impressed by Zhu's performance and in 1992 he engineered his promotion to the position of Vice Premier specialising in economic issues. He reported to Li Peng. Zhu would not have been Li's choice. He was a reformer in the style of Deng Xiaoping, and Li and Zhu seem to have had a frosty relationship for much of the time. But Zhu was hard to push aside because each difficult assignment he was handed, he handled with skill and speed. He sorted out the state-owned enterprise bad loans problem, then he managed China's response to the global recession of the early 1990s. Next, in response to a critical shortfall in central government revenues, he restructured the national tax system, completing that job in 1994. So by the time the reform of the state-owned enterprises landed in his lap, he was an experienced problem solver and policy maker and he knew his way around Beijing's corridors of power.

It took a year or more of discussion and horse-trading before Zhu came up with a workable plan. It was approved at the 15th Communist Party Congress which was held in Beijing in September 1997. In the characteristically Chinese fashion, the policy was described with a slogan: "grasp the large, release the small". It meant that the larger state-owned enterprises would remain in government hands, and the smaller ones would be either privatized, handed over to local governments, or shut down altogether. Of the sector's 150 million workers, the small ones employed about 70 million. So the reforms meant that 70 million workers and their families were about to be "released" from the protective cocoon of guaranteed government employment.[56]

That was not all. The second part of the reform was that all of the state-owned enterprises, both large and small, were to relinquish their welfare obligations. No longer would they have to provide schooling, health care and retirement benefits. Neither would they have to provide housing for their employees. Gone too was the guaranteed employment, even in those which were remaining under central government control. The policy was clear: state-owned businesses large and small were now going to be run as businesses, not as Mao-era social welfare projects.

There was still more to the reform package. Now that the state-owned enterprises were to cease funding the hospitals and schools, there was to be a tax levied on each worker to make up the shortfall. The workers were to be taxed in order to pay for the social services they had previously been given for free. As for the company housing, it was to be sold off. Each apartment would first be offered to the occupant, and if that offer was not taken up, it would be sold on the open market. The sale of housing was to be done at very low prices, and where the occupants did not have the savings to afford a cash payment, a low interest loan was available. The requirement which came along with these loans was that the new owners could not sell for five years.

The reforms were enacted in 1998. In the first year some six million workers lost their jobs. In the second year a further five million were lost. This meant that in two years about one in fifteen workers in the state-owned, and formerly state-owned, sector had lost their jobs. It could have been a lot worse. Yet it was enough to cause concern. Consumer spending slowed down in the cities. This was not only due to the retrenchments. There was also the fear of retrenchment, and then there were the additional expenses in the form of mortgage and welfare tax payments. Added to that, families now started to put money aside for the times when they would get sick or lose their jobs. The average household savings rate, already high, rose higher still.

Zhu Rongji's reforms drove a rapid transformation of the small state-owned enterprises.[57] Being small, they did not have the production capacity or political clout to protect their turf, and were now faced with an adapt-or-die imperative. It did not turn out to be the disaster everyone feared. For the most part, the companies adapted. For those that did not, their laid-off workers were mostly welcomed by the private sector. Their better training made them a useful addition to the ranks of the unskilled migrant workers.

Overall, the whole process was an unexpected success.[58] China's annual GDP growth barely faltered. In 1997, the last year before the reforms, it had been 8.8%, the next year it fell to 7.8%, and then it dropped down to 7.1% in 1999. That was as low as it got. Thing got much better from there. Because as the new decade dawned it would soon become clear that Zhu Rong-Ji's reforms were going to be more far-reaching than anyone anticipated. It was an unintended consequence, but it turned out that the privatisation of China's state-owned housing would set the foundation for ten years of Chinese urban development on a scale which the world had never before seen.

Chapter 4

FROM 2000 TO 2020

The Housing Boom

By the time Zhu Rong-Ji was announcing his reforms, housing in China's cities had become a real problem. The state-owned businesses were not making any money, so there was not much in the kitty for the building of new apartments for their growing workforce. There was not even much available for the maintenance of the existing stock. When accommodation had to be built it was the bare minimum quality and size. Even then the financial burden on the state-owned companies was such that taking the responsibilty for housing away from them was the main driver behind Zhu's decision to privatise state-owned housing.

It was not only the state-owned housing which was a problem. There was not enough housing of any kind.[59] Any spare capacity had disappeared as soon as the migrant workers started to move to the cities. Through the 1990s they had come in droves, and they needed somewhere to live. The foreign-owned companies managed this by building dormitories and food halls for their workers. There was not much privacy but at least it was shelter. However most of the home-grown Chinese companies which were setting up in the cities had little money, nor had they any guaranteed future, so they did not build anything to house or feed the workers. The workers were left to fend for themselves. Some slept on the company premises. Others, especially those with families, found rental accommodation wherever it was available. Still others grouped together and erected makeshift accommodation, creating what were in effect shanty towns.

The lack of urban housing had long been a fact of life in China. When Deng Xiaoping came to power he had initiated an apartment building drive as part of his effort to improve living standards. Such was its scale that contemporary accounts describe it as a housing boom. In some cities the floorspace built during first half of the 1980s was equal to the entire amount built between 1950 and 1980. The aim had been to increase the average per capita floorspace to five square metres, up from the Mao era average of four. It was no doubt a welcome improvement for the workers but the cost was prohibitive and still the average standard of housing was abysmal.

Experiments with housing privatisation had begun in the mid 1980s. They failed because rents were so low that hardly anyone thought it worthwhile to take up the offer to buy their apartment. Tienanmen Square and the rise of the conservatives had put a stop to such experiments. The notion of privately-owned housing was a particular dislike of theirs.

The push towards privately-funded and privately-owned housing began again in 1993. Shanghai and several other cities authorised the construction of housing for private sale. Houses built for private sale were larger and had much better facilities than those built by the state-owned enterprises. These were for the wealthy businesspeople, and by the mid 1990s there were enough of them to make it a viable market. But it remained small. The great majority of urban housing was state-owned, overcrowded and poorly maintained. That was the state of things when Zhu Rong-Ji announced his reforms.

Between 1999 and 2001 all of this rundown housing fell into the hands of private owners.[60] Many workers made the decision to buy their apartment when it was offered. Those apartments which the occupiers did not buy were sold off either to another family or, less often, to privately-owned companies. Those apartments were then rented back to the current occupants. It was inevitable that the rents would be higher than before. This was because the previous rents had been too low to pay even for basic maintenance let alone for any significant upgrade.

After a year or two the rents became even higher. This was because the lack of housing meant that when an apartment was listed as vacant there was a lot of interest. It was a landlord's market. There was a lot of pent-up demand just waiting for new apartments. It did not take a financial genius to recognise that there was money to be made in building apartments and selling them. Once this recognition sunk in, it took no time at all to launch a host of construction companies. And so began the great China housing boom.[61]

All construction has to begin with the acquisition of some land. In China, all land belongs to the state. In the case of city apartment buildings, the relevant owner of the land (thanks to reforms announced in 1994 by Zhu Rong-Ji) was the city government.[62] The first step, therefore, for a company intent on building an apartment block was to approach the city authorities and ask for a parcel of land. At the beginning of the housing boom the land was still fairly readily available within the defined city limits, but competition for it was fierce. The developers soon found that their prospects were enhanced if they were prepared to pay something "under the table" to one or two of the more influential city officials. Corruption, already a serious blight in the city governments, became a way of life.

Another thing needs to be said about land in China: most cities are surrounded by fertile farm land, and farm land in China was already in short supply. This being the case, that land was off-limits for building developers. So there was an imperative to build up, not out. In this way Chinese cities became a forest of scaffolding and cranes, as the construction began of high rise apartment blocks. Prior to the housing reforms, a city apartment block might be three floors high. Now with land becoming increasingly expensive, in the early years of the housing boom ten to fifteen floors became the standard. They became higher as the years went by.

From the beginning, these new privately-built apartments were far more spacious than the state-owned ones. In state-owned housing, per capita floorspace might be ten square metres, often it was less. In the new apartments, 25 square metres was typical in the biggest cities. It went up to 30, and even 35, square metres, in the smaller cities where land was more readily available. The apartments were also self-contained. There was no sharing of washing and cooking facilities.

This being the case, they cost a lot more to buy than the state-owned apartments, which had in any case been offered at knock-down prices. But Chinese families were tired of living in cramped accommodation where they had to queue for the toilet and the kitchen. Many of these families had money. Firstly, they had been saving for years, as was the Chinese habit. Secondly, wages were rising along with the roaring urban economy. Thirdly many of them now owned a formerly government-owned apartment whose value was rising all the time. They could sell it, or rent it out. With that additional money, along with their savings and higher salary, they could afford the downpayment on the new apartment and the repayments on the loan.

With this dynamic propelling it along, the construction of high rise apartments blocks consumed the cities. The migrant workers kept arriving, adding more fuel to the fire. Between 2000 and 2010, the population of China's cities rose by 200 million people. Even had the population stayed steady, there would have been a huge increase in residential construction because the existing housing was in such poor condition. With the urban population increasing by nearly 50% in ten years, it led to a housing construction boom on an epic scale.[62]

By the middle of the decade the land in the cities was becoming increasingly hard to find. But the demand for it was just getting started. There were thousands of apartment blocks still to be built, as well as city office blocks, shopping malls and ever more factories. They could all be built higher still, but it was inevitable that the cities would start to spread. For this to happen, farm land had to be encroached upon.

City governments did have the power to requisition farm land for development, but for a long time they hesitated. For one thing, the requisitioning power was only supposed to be used in extraordinary circumstances, and even then only with appropriate compensation for the dispossessed farmers. But as the pressure increased from developers and investors, the farm land which surrounded the cities was the only option for expansion. The hesitation fell away when developers began to offer ever more in the way of "special payments" to the city officials. In return, the city officials began to discover a whole lot of "extraordinary circumstances" reasons to requisition the farm land. As for compensation for the farmers whose land was requisitioned, the city authorities were not very generous.

In this way, when the housing boom really began to ramp up after 2004, large swathes of prime farm land were bulldozed.[63] In total, in the years between 2000 and 2010, the built-up area occupied by China's cities went from about 17,000 square kilometres to nearly 30,000. By the end of the decade there was twice as much floorspace in China's cities as there had been at the beginning.

Workshop of the World

The housing boom drove, and was driven by, a surge in manufacturing which by 2010 had propelled China to the position of largest manufacturing nation on earth. The country was already a manufacturer of global importance by the end of the 1990s. In fact, by that time it was the largest manufacturing-for-export nation. It dominated the global manufacture of toys, plastic goods, and simple electric appliances such as fans and bedside lights. It also produced a big share of the white goods and more complex electrical items such as TVs and mobile phones. To give some statistics: in 2001, China manufactured one quarter of the world's washing machines, one third of its air conditioners, microwaves and colour TVs, half of its cameras and phones, and more than two thirds of its DVD players.[64] A lot of this was for domestic consumption, but the majority was for export.

In the early 2000s, goods for export were mostly manufactured by foreign-owned companies. The majority of these factories were not really manufacturing operations. They were assembly operations, receiving imported components, putting them together and then exporting the finished product. A good example of this was Foxconn,[65] a Taiwanese-owned firm which had established its first small facility in Shenzhen in 1988. By 1998 it had two sprawling factories making mobile phones and portable computers, one each in Shenzhen and Shanghai. They imported most of the high tech components which went into them, using their Chinese factories for assembly and packaging. Foxconn was one of the larger foreign-owned export-manufacturing companies, but there were very many smaller companies doing the same sort of thing.

The home-grown Chinese manufacturers did not have much share in the export trade. There were two reasons for this. In the higher value items such as white goods, electronics and machine tools they did not have the skills or equipment to manufacture products good enough for the consumers in the USA, Japan and western Europe. In the lower value items, such as textiles, clothing and cheap electric goods, the western countries had applied quotas and tariffs in order to protect their own industries.

So as the 1990s came to an end, manufacturing in China could be considered as consisting of two distinct groups. There were the foreign-owned plants producing for export. They were almost all located in the Special Economic Zones. Then there were the Chinese-owned plants which produced goods primarily for the domestic market. They were mostly located in large industrial parks elsewhere in the coastal cities.

They, in turn, could be divided into two groups. The first group was the privately-owned plants. They were usually manufacturing low value products which needed only basic technical knowledge and equipment. The second was the state-owned plants. They were mainly producing the higher value goods which needed a higher level of technical knowledge and a more elaborate and heavier duty set of factory equipment.

This was not a picture which satisfied Zhu Rong-Ji and the rest of the senior leadership. They wanted the export manufacturing to be done by Chinese companies. They were well aware of the way in which China's near neighbours had managed to develop so quickly. Japan, Taiwan and South Korea had all grown on the back of a domestically-owned manufacturing industry making products for western markets. The Party leadership knew that that was where China had to be. It was not enough to be a host to foreign-owned assembly plants. They were a stepping stone. The real goal was to develop a domestically-owned manufacturing base which exported to the western countries. So the Chinese leadership set about trying to build one.

To explain how they did it, it is once again useful to go back a bit in history. China had from the beginning of the reform era benefitted from a supportive United States. Whilst many on the anti-communist side of American politics opposed providing any support to them, that group was always out-numbered by the larger group which saw China's economic progress as a benefit to the west.

That said, the Chinese knew that support from United States was not exactly guaranteed and they set about looking for a more permanent base on which to build. This was the rationale which drove China to apply for membership in the GATT, which was at the time the body which set the rules for world trade. The first approach was made in the mid 1980s. The application was refused because of China's high tariffs and its high degree of government intervention in the economy. The Party leadership persisted, and was refused again and again, until the GATT was replaced by the World Trade Organisation, or WTO, in 1995. When they applied for membership of this new organisation, they were refused once again.

The stalemate was broken in 1998 when Li Peng was replaced by Zhu Rong-Ji as China's chief economic policy-maker. Zhu set his sights on membership of the WTO in the belief that it was the best and quickest way to build a strong domestic manufacturing capability. He lowered tariffs, reduced the role of the government in the economy and agreed to a range of conditions which would open up the Chinese domestic market to foreign banks, telecoms and retail companies. Having made these concessions, China became a member of the WTO in December 2001.[66]

The gaining of WTO membership would have been a benefit to China in any event. It turned out to be much better than that. This is because, at the same time as China was entering the WTO, four developments in the wider world were gathering pace. Together these developments created a huge opportunity for any country in the right position to benefit from them. China was in that right position. It meant that its accession to WTO membership delivered an extraordinary windfall.

The first of the developments was the rise in the importance of intangible services in global trade. For millenia, trade between countries had mainly been in tangible products like food, clothing and minerals. Things had changed by the 1990s. The western economies were now predominantly services economies. They specialised in products like financial services, software creation, education, health care and technical design of all kinds, and they wanted to trade these services. World trade was at the time governed by the GATT. In place since the end of World War II, the GATT dealt only in tangible goods like grain, light bulbs and cars. It was no longer serving the western countries very well.

As a result it was scrapped and replaced by the World Trade Organisation, which was established in 1995. The WTO was designed to govern trade in all products: tangible goods, intangible services and intellectual property. Armed with this better trade framework, many of the western nations, especially the USA, were now prepared to open their borders to unimpeded competition from low cost foreign countries. It was done on the understanding that their banking, telecom, education and other service sectors would be allowed unimpeded access into those same foreign countries. It was a deal which, as it turned out, was far more beneficial to the low cost manufacturing countries than it was to the high tech services-providing countries.

The second development which benefitted China was the fact that beginning in the mid 1990s there began across much of the western world a period of unusually rapid increases in house prices. This rise brought with it a rising appetite for consumption – including for manufactured goods - on the part of the home owners. Otherwise known as the "wealth effect", this rising appetite was fully in evidence during the five years which followed China's entry to the WTO.

The third development which benefitted China was the Asian Crisis. This is the name given to the financial crash which occurred in 1997 in the industrialising South East Asian nations of Thailand, Indonesia and Malaysia. These countries had enjoyed ten years of strong economic progress, in part because they were the countries into which Japanese manufacturers were relocating their factories as they searched for lower costs. They were good years for these countries but they did not put in the needed infrastructure development. As a result, manufacturing development ground to halt and investment money was instead funnelled into real estate development. Land prices rose. The crash came in the middle of 1997. Even when they had recovered, Thailand, Indonesia and Malaysia never returned to their pre-crash rates of growth. The world had lost confidence in their economic management. It was a good outcome for China because, just as it was preparing its own domestic companies to compete for export sales, three of its most formidable competitors were greatly diminished in their ability to compete.

The fourth and final development was the tech revolution. Starting in the late 1990s the computer went from being a help in the office and at home to being a social phenomenon. Everyone from primary schoolers to their grandparents now needed all sorts of communication devices which a few years before they could not even have imagined. It drove a very steep climb in global demand for laptop computers, smart phones and everything else that assisted the consumer to be on-line at all times. The tech revolution created a huge demand for entirely new classes of consumer goods.

So just as China was gearing up to help its domestic manufacturers break into global markets, it found itself almost alone on the world stage as a reliable, low cost manufacturing location in the midst of an unprecedented global surge in demand for low-cost manufactured goods, and an increasingly liberal approach to trade in those goods.

The first impact of these four developments was that China became an even more attractive location for western manufacturers looking to reduce their costs and expand their factories. Attracting them was a task for which China's coastal cities were well-prepared. They had by then twenty years of experience in making things easy for foreigners to set-up shop. They had millions of disciplined migrant workers willing to work for low wages. When those all had jobs, there were millions more ready and willing. The city governments owned all the land, so clearing the way for industrial parks was just a matter of finding enough bulldozers. Development permits? No problem. There was no need to worry about local residents picketing a construction site. Firstly, there was a great deal of public support for the developments, and secondly, to paraphrase Deng Xiaoping, "the beauty of one-Party government is that you just have to decide what you want to do, then you do it."

As for building the roads, ports, airports, power lines, street lights, communications networks and everything else that the foreign companies needed, the Chinese city authorities developed a speed and efficiency in the construction of infrastructure that was something other countries could only marvel at.

This makes China's success in attracting foreign investment sound easy, which of course it was not. There was one issue in particular which often caused problems, and that was finding the money to pay for it all. But eventually that was solved too. Innovative financial management became a way of life in the city governments of the day.

There developed two main centres of manufacturing-for-export factories. The largest of them was Shanghai and the surrounding cities.[67] They formed a great expanse of industrialisation, which was burning so much coal and petroleum fuel that as the years went on smog became a serious problem and blue sky became a rare sight. The other main centre was the Pearl River Delta.[68] The sky in this region was rarely blue either. Together, Shanghai and the Pearl River Delta were responsible for making about 60% of all of China's exported manufactured goods.

Western manufacturers kept arriving throughout the decade, setting-up factories for export manufacture. What about the China's own domestic companies? How did they go with building export sales? Money for investment was no problem. The Chinese government poured money into the state-owned companies which had the capability for the task. The harder part was developing the equipment designs and the technical know-how to make products of a quality similar to established western brands.

It was here that China earned a bad name for itself. How much outright theft of intellectual property there really was is an open question, but certainly a fair bit of it went on. The Chinese government also engaged in strong-arm tactics by requiring foreign companies to enter joint-ventures which stipulated that the foreign company had to handover some of its secrets to its partner.

That played a part in helping the domestic Chinese companies to build their exports so quickly, but its benefit is often exaggerated. The bigger part of the home-grown Chinese company's export growth came through their skill both in keeping costs down and in developing with remarkable speed a western-style focus on quality. Over the decade, Chinese domestic manufacturers increased their export output even faster than did foreign-owned manufacturers.

With foreign companies moving in in such numbers, and home-grown companies building their overseas customer base so rapidly, it seemed by 2010 that the rest of the world had out-sourced its manufacturing to China. In that year China produced nine out of every ten computers manufactured on the planet. That came to a total of 360 million Made in China computers,[69] up from less than 7 million in 2000. It produced eight out of every ten of the world's airconditioners, which came to a total of 109 million, up from the about 20 million which were made in China ten years earlier. It produced seven out of every ten mobile phones, which meant that Chinese factories produced 1.1 billion of them, up from 50 million in 2000. The list goes on. Two out of every three pairs of the world's shoes were made in China, as were four out of every five umbrellas. The country totally dominated the new industry of roof-top solar panels. Even the automobile assembly lines were shifting to China. One in every six of the world's motor cars was made in the country in 2010.

China had become the Workshop of the World.[70] Not everyone agreed. According to some, it was not much of a workshop at all, it was really only a glorified assembly line.[71] But the figures tell a different story. In 2010, China's share of global manufacturing value-added was equal to that of the United States, well above that of Japan, and more than double that of Germany. It was a manufacturer in its own right. It dominated the global production of low-complexity goods. Meanwhile the United States, Japan and Germany fought it out for dominance in high-complexity manufactured goods. China would challenge for a share in that market over the next ten years.

Paying For It All

The simultaneous and very rapid development of both manufacturing industry and urban residential accommodation inevitably put a strain on the economy. One remarkable thing about the Chinese achievement was that its economy did not break down under this strain. Instead, seemingly without effort, China managed to supply all the people, land, materials, fuel, infrastructure and capital to allow the country's expansion of construction and production to increase at a rate of about 10% per year for three decades and more.

The availability of people, as has already been discussed, was for China the easy part. There was something approaching a bottomless pit of workers just waiting in the farming regions. The availability of land has also been discussed. That was more of a problem, but China chose to sacrifice farming land to make room for the factories and high rises. As regards the availability of minerals and fuel, that will be discussed in the next book in this series. Which leaves the matters of infrastructure and finance.

To support the great wave of construction and production which was unleashed in the wake of the Zhu Rong-Ji reforms, China needed a very extensive program of infrastructure building. Before discussing how they paid for it, is worthwhile briefly describing the scale of the construction which happened during those years. Between 2002 and 2008, the country's electrical generation capacity doubled and the length of its highway network tripled, increasing from 19,000 kilometres to 62,000. The railway network was the laggard, adding just 20% to its length. That amounted to a total additional length of 22,000 kilometres, including 5,000 kilometres of high-speed railway.

If the railway was the laggard, China's port system was the star of the infrastructure show. There are two basic types of port: those designed for handling bulk materials like iron ore, coal and bauxite, and those designed for handling shipping containers. Between 1998 and 2008, throughput of China's bulk handling ports increased fivefold. The ports of Ningbo, Tianjin, Tangshan and Suzhou became the largest in the world for the handling of incoming bulk materials. As for the container ports, their throughput went up by a factor of ten. In 1998, China had three container ports in the global top 20. Ten years later, it had nine. Shanghai which was ranked number 10 in the world in 1998, had risen to number 2 by 2008. Shenzhen which had been at number 15 was at number 4. The container port of Ningbo (near Shanghai) which had not even existed in 1990 was ranked number 8 in the world in 2008, making it larger than Rotterdam, Europe's busiest container port.[72]

There was far more infrastructure development than that. One more statistic, already stated in the previous section, will help capture the scale: between 2000 and 2010, China's urban built-up area nearly doubled and its urban floorspace did double. Which meant that the country's urban water and sewage systems, telecommunications networks, retail areas and all the rest of the city facilities doubled in size in just ten years. Which placed a very heavy demand on the public treasury. So where did all the money come from? Here again, to provide some context, it is useful to briefly recount the history of China's management of government finances in the reform era.

Throughout the 1980s and the early 1990s, the central government in Beijing paid for most of the infrastructure built anywhere in China. For this, they relied on taxation revenue. The tax take consisted of a 55% tax on the profits of state-owned enterprises, a 10% value-added tax and a set of duties on imported goods. The system did not work very well.[73] At least not from the point of view of the central government. By the early 1990s their taxation revenue had basically dried up.

The root of the problem was that the taxes were collected by the city authorities, and they could not be trusted. Take the 55% profit tax. The city authorities had got into the habit of doing sweetheart deals with the state-owned enterprises in their jurisdiction. The city would give the enterprise a tax holiday (for some made-up reason), and a good portion of this tax break would then be paid back to the city as a kick-back. In this way the city collected a good amount of tax which it otherwise probably would not have received, and the central government missed out. As for the 10% VAT revenues and the import duties, the situation was worse. The city authorities more or less stopped collecting them. After all, with most of the money going back to the central government, why would they go to the trouble?

The result was that by 1993, the city authorities were doing quite well and the central government was in a very poor financial position. Despite a decade of 10% economic growth per year, their tax take had not increased since 1980.

Enter the great reformer, Zhu Rong-Ji. He restructured the system so that the central government itself employed the tax collectors for the VAT. For good measure, he raised the VAT rate to 17%. The VAT collectors were also charged with collecting the profit tax from the larger state-owned enterprises. To make it easier to collect, Zhu reduced the profit tax from 55% to 30%.[74] Both tax takes were sent directly to Beijing. As for the profit tax payable by the smaller state-owned enterprises and the private companies, Zhu left it up to the provincial authorities to collect. They were allowed to keep it.

Once those reforms had been enacted, the central government was collecting, and keeping, two thirds of the total national tax take. It was back in the black. The attentive reader will have noticed that the city authorities, once central players in the tax collection process, had been cut out of the process altogether. They were now in the red.

Zhu knew that the city governments had plenty of clever operators in their employ who would try every trick in the book to claw back their losses, so he included in his tax reform a clause which forbade the local authorities to waive any company's taxes or to raise new taxes without Beijing's approval. Nor could they get bank loans without permission. They were however allowed one new freedom: they were permitted to control the allocation of the urban land, and to lease it to the recipients at whatever rates they saw fit. The phrase "give them an inch and they'll take a mile" comes to mind.

It turned out that the power to allocate and lease land was a financial bonanza for China's city governments. Instead of being losers from Zhu's tax reform, as it seemed initially, the city authorities turned out to be big winners. Urban land, as they discovered, was worth a lot more in revenue than whatever tax takings they had lost. Developers would pay big money for a prime location, with the result that those cities with plenty of vacant land were soon wealthy. None got wealthier than Shanghai. Pudong was a gold mine for them.

Even for those cities with little vacant land, which sooner or later was every city, there was always the surrounding farm land. The urban authorities soon discovered another thing: they could get that farm land for close to nothing. All it took was some heavy-handed tactics. In this way, it could be said, that the great infrastructure and housing building booms which followed Zhu's late 1990s reforms were, in significant part, funded by dispossessing the farmers who worked the land on the fringes of the cities.

The Great Stimulus Package

The Chinese economy was the wonder of the world in the first decade of the 21st century. It seemed unstoppable, its GDP increasing at an average rate of 10% per year, year after year. It was already a very large economy, and by adding that amount of economic activity each year it seemed as if the Chinese government was run by some new breed of economic wizards.

In contrast the western countries were in the slow lane. If a western country achieved annual GDP growth of 3% that counted as a good year. In some years, growth fell to just 1%. Nevertheless, in the housing sector, some of the western countries were experiencing impressive growth. House prices in the USA rose at 10% per year between 2000 and 2006. The homeowners, seeing their houses appreciate in value so quickly, began to consider themselves wealthy. So they started borrowing at levels not seen before. Banks, seeing an apparently unending rise in house prices, began granting mortgages to all comers, even to those who obviously could not afford the repayments. The banks then packaged these mortgages into financial black boxes and sold them to other banks as low risk securities.

That was fine, as long as the house prices kept rising. Unfortunately, they started falling in mid-2006. The fall was gentle at first, then there was a big drop in mid-2007. The banks now started taking a closer look at their piles of "low risk" mortgage-based securities. They found that far from being low risk, they were of unknown, and quite possibly very high, risk. When the reality of that sank in, there was a rush for the door. With everyone wanting to sell them, the mortgage-backed securities plummeted in value. Confidence in banks evaporated because no-one really knew where the securities were and what they contained, and that loss of confidence spread throughout the economy. Global stock markets lost 50% of their value between July and October 2008. Many of the western countries sank into recession. It was called the Global Financial Crisis.[75]

China had very few of these dubious securities so the damage to its banking system was minimal. But its stock exchanges were brutalised. Hong Kong's Hang Seng Index lost 60% by the end of 2008. The Shanghai Composite Index lost 70%. As the recession started to take hold in western countries, China's trade revenues looked like they also were going to be brutalised. Imports for the assembly-for-export plants plunged in October 2008. It was only a matter of time before the exports followed suit. Alarm bells started ringing in Beijing.

To consider what to do about it, a State Council meeting was held in early November 2008. The meeting ended with a dramatic decision. The Chinese government would pump $600 billion into the economy in order to replace the jobs which would probably be lost by closures of the assembly-for-export factories. One quarter of the money was to be put towards the rebuilding of Sichuan following the earthquake of May 2008. Another quarter would go to the construction of the national high-speed rail network. The rest was to be spent on a wide variety of projects including highways, standard railways, dams, bridges, hospitals, solar and wind farms, and low-cost housing developments. All of them were "shovel ready" projects. The key for selecting any project was that it could be implemented quickly. As a widely circulated memo put it: "The absolutely most important work is to urgently implement the centre's increased investment measures so as to increase demand."[76]

It seemed to work. Yes, economic growth slowed to 6.9% in the last quarter of 2008 and was even lower in the first quarter of 2009. And exports fell by about 20% in 2009 versus 2008. But all that was to be expected. The important thing was that an upwards trend in the unemployment was averted. It scarcely moved. By the end of 2009 the danger had passed. Export shipments recovered somewhat in 2010 and, with the stimulus measures in full cry, the economy returned to rude health.

But something had changed. The economy had not really bounced back to where it was.[77] The export engine of growth had slowed down. The big fall in exports in 2009 was never really regained. Exports were still a large part of the economy but they were no longer a growing part. This was, to a large extent, due to the fact that the customers for those exports were now living in economies which were gripped by recession.

But there was more to it than that. For one thing, there were the rising wages of the Chinese workers. China's low cost advantage was progressively being lost. For another thing, there was, for the first time, some serious political pushback in western countries against China's low-cost exports.

There had always been political pushback on the China trade. But it is surprising how little pushback there had been given that the western countries had been for ten years importing far more from China than they were exporting to it. Especially when that gap was widening each year. It was not supposed to be that way. With China in the WTO, its markets were meant to open up. The advanced countries were supposed to be exporting services and high-level manufactured goods to China while the less-complex manufactured goods were supposed to go from China to the advanced countries. It never quite worked out that way. The flow was very lopsided in favour of China. When times were good, this could be tolerated. Now that times were bad, the issue received a lot more attention.

The overall result was that the export trade which had served China so well since the early 1980s was losing steam. Because this threatened a lot of people's livelihoods, the government had to respond. One way of doing that was to encourage greater consumer spending within China itself. After all, the goods being exported were mainly for consumer and household use. If Chinese consumers could be encouraged to open their wallets, it would just be a matter of shipping the goods inland instead of overseas.

For this to work the Chinese people had to have money to spend. They also had to have a willingness to spend it. This required not only higher wages, it also required that the Chinese people had a better social safety net so they felt more secure. The insecurity of the average Chinese household was reflected in the savings rate: it was the highest of any large country in the world. The insecurity was most prominent among the migrant workers. There were some 250 million of them and they lived in permanent insecurity. That is not a good basis upon which to build increased consumer spending.

All of this was known to China's leadership, and had long been known. The successors to Jiang Zemin and Zhu Rong-Ji were Hu Jintao and Wen Jiabao. They came to power in 2002. Well before the GFC, Hu and Wen had shown that they were well aware of the need to create a consumer society which felt secure enough to spend its money. The two of them had given many speeches on the subject, and launched programs to address it. But nothing much had been achieved. In part it was because there was not the urgency. In part also it was because Hu and Wen were not in the same class as the great reformers who had preceded them.

Average wages did rise steadily between 2000 and 2010 which meant that the average Chinese family had more to spend. But instead of spending it, they saved it. This was probably due to the demands of home ownership. To buy a new home, the buyer had to pay a large deposit, which had to be funded from savings. The savings rate in 2010 was 52%, and it fell to 46% over the next five years. Whichever of those numbers is chosen, the Chinese people were in saving mode not spending mode.

With exports declining and consumers not spending, it was clear that some other engine of growth was needed for the economy, and the engine to which the government turned was infrastructure spending. It had worked in 2009. For this reason, when the original GFC stimulus program was completed, the government decided to keep it going.

There were two ways it could be funded. The central government could use its own cash reserves, or it could encourage the spending to be done by local governments and state-owned enterprises.

The Party leadership chose the second way. To allow it to happen they had to loosen the once very tight reins over bank lending. It will be recalled that Zhu Rong-Ji had, back in 1994, removed the right for city governments to borrow money. Now those same city governments were given licence to borrow as they saw fit, as long as those borrowings were guaranteed by urban land leases. State-owned enterprises were also given the right to borrow as they saw fit, and their borrowings were not really guaranteed by anything. The point of it all was to encourage investment, and the point of that was to create economic growth. After all, there was nothing else driving it.

It worked quite well, and spending on infrastructure and urban construction, funded by easy money, has been the main driver of Chinese economic growth ever since.[78] Infrastructure building has reached new heights. The national highway network doubled in size between 2008 and 2017, increasing from 62,000 kilometres to 131,000 kilometres. Over the same time there has been a surge in railway construction the likes of which has never before been seen in China. Over 40,000 kilometres of track has been laid, which is about half as much as was laid in the 58 years between 1950 and 2008. Much of it was for the high-speed rail network. Construction at the ports also continued apace. In 2017, China had seven of the world's top ten container ports. Added to the mix has been the Belt and Road Initiative, which has the potential to be the biggest infrastructure building program of all.

Urban construction has plateaued but at the already very high levels of the last years of the housing boom. The money spent on high rise buildings, factories and other fixed assets since 2010 is four times the amount which was spent during the frenetic years between 2000 and 2010. One driver is the steady stream of new people still coming into the cities. This has averaged twenty million per year for the last 20 years but it is no longer increasing. Not to worry. Property developers have kept on building new apartments anyway, with the result that residential construction is often well ahead of actual demand for apartments. Entire satellite cities have been constructed, complete with high rise apartment blocks and shopping malls, with no-one living in them. To date, experience shows that these apartments and shopping areas do in the end attract buyers and tenants. Even so, these so-called Ghost Cities are a sign of how important a relentless, keep-on-building construction industry has become in the economy.

In this way the Chinese economy has, for the last five years, depended on infrastructure building and urban housing construction. This is a risky strategy, and in any case is not going to last forever. The infrastructure projects which are being built are less necessary than they once were, and some have the appearance of being built solely to create employment. Housing construction will continue at a good pace because there are many families yet to leave the farms. But it has lost its potency as a driver of the economy. All of which means that the Chinese economy needs a new driver. There is only one such driver, and that is the Chinese consumer.

Chapter 5

CHINA TO 2030

The Next Leap Forward

It is now time to consider where the Chinese economy may go from here. To assist with this analysis, a framework has been developed. It maps out a continuous pathway of development which all countries follow on their journey from being a farming economy to being a fully-industrialised and urbanised economy.

The notion that there is such a common pathway was first systematically explored in a book, *The Stages of Economic Growth*,[79] written by the economist Walt Whitman Rostow and published in 1960. In the book he proposed a model which consists of a sequence of stages which nations pass through in their journey from being an agricultural to an urbanised "mass consumption" economy.

A similar model is used here to explain where China is in its economic development, and where it needs to go. The model goes like this: when countries are moving from being agricultural economies to being urbanised, services-focussed economies they pass through two stages of industrial development. The first of these involves a lot of investment in city building and factory construction. It is called the Urban stage. The second involves the building of a consumer society on this foundation of factories and cities. It is called the Household stage. There is a third stage, which the Advanced Countries are now in. It is called the Innovative Services stage. This model is explained in more detail in the third book in this series, *The Path of Industrialisation: 1880 to 2050.*[80]

In terms of this framework, China in 2020 is at the end of the Urban stage and is now attempting to make the transition into the Household stage.

The Urban stage is typically a thirty- or forty-year period during which a good portion of the farm population shifts to the cities attracted by the better-paying manufacturing and services jobs which are on offer. At the beginning of the stage, about 4 in every 5 people live on the land or earn their living in nearby small towns. By the end of the stage, only about 1 in every 2 people are still in living in those circumstances. The rest of them have moved, or migrated if the Chinese term is to be used, to the cities.

The farm work being done at the beginning of the stage is a labour-intensive occupation which has relatively low productivity. By moving to the cities and working in factories and services occupations, the migrant farm workers greatly increase their productivity. This is why they are paid more. At the same time, those left behind also increase their productivity because they are using labour-saving devices as well as improved farming techniques such as fertiliser, irrigation and improved seed types. They too earn more.

This shift of people to the cities not only provides a workforce for manufacturing and services jobs, it also creates demand for housing, consumer goods and urban services. The construction of infrastructure and residential housing becomes a big part of the economy, and the cities grow in size. It is a self-reinforcing process because as more people arrive in the cities, more housing and goods are needed, resulting in more construction and expansion of the factories.

The trigger for the Urban stage is typically a mixture of push and pull – that is, people are pushed off the land because they are no longer needed, and they are pulled off the land by the availability of jobs in the towns and cities. The "push" happens when farming becomes more productive and yields per hectare increase, thereby creating a surplus of workers and food. The "pull" happens when there is increased demand for manufactured goods and that creates jobs for people in urban factories. This is the dynamic which drove the Chinese economy in the 1980s and the process continued to reinforce itself, ever more strongly, over the next two decades. The strength of the "pull" in China was greatly enhanced when the export manufacturing sector took off in the 1990s.

One of the characteristics of the Urban stage is that it tends to result in a great disparity in income levels. The people who own the businesses become wealthy. Part of the reason is that they do not have to pay their workers very much, just enough to make it worthwhile for them to leave their very low paid jobs on the farms. It is also usually the case that the government has not yet put in place a welfare system for the common people, so they do not have much of a social safety net. As a result, the common people tend to save their meagre earnings as a cushion against future misfortune. These savings are an important ingredient in the Urban stage, because they are put towards investment in infrastructure building.

The Chinese economy has had a very successful journey through the Urban stage of economic development. But the Urban stage does not last forever, and China has reached the end of it. It is now time for it to shift an economic gear, and move into the Household stage. This means, to put it into economist-speak, shifting the weight of spending in the economy from investment to consumption.

For a country to enter the Household stage and progress through it, workers have to earn more and be confident to spend those earnings. This requires several things to happen:

- New technology must be introduced right across the economy – in agriculture, manufacturing and services. This raises worker productivity, allowing them to be paid more.

- The distribution of wealth in the economy must be made more equitable, an outcome typically achieved through tax reform and wage rises.
- A social safety net must be put in place to give workers the confidence to spend more than they save.

These three shifts – higher productivity, a broader distribution of the wealth it creates, and a social safety net - do wonders for the economy. They created the conditions for the post-war boom in the countries of North America and Western Europe. It is this prosperous stage of development on which China is now attempting to embark.

Making this transition is never easy – for any country - because it requires giving to the common people much more of the power and wealth in the economy. Obviously this means that those who already have the power and wealth have to give it up. That meets with plenty of resistance. Especially in a country like China where there is an entrenched authoritarian government. For this reason, and many others, it cannot be assumed that China will successfully achieve this transition.

In fact, more countries fail than succeed. When, in the 1920s, it came time for the United States and the countries of Western Europe to make the transition, it looked at first like they had done it easily. That was the Roaring Twenties. But they had not restructured their economies so as to make it a sustainable transition and the result was the Great Depression. Eventually they did make it, in the aftermath of the Second World War. The destruction and trauma of the war was such that, when it was over, restructuring the rules of the economy was relatively easy.

The Soviet Union did not manage the transition at all. It entered the Urban stage in the late 1920s when Josef Stalin decided his country had to reach Great Power status within ten years or it would perish at the hands of foreign invaders. The Soviet Union's progress through the Urban stage was, partly thanks to Stalin's relentless pushing, done at a speed which made other countries take notice. Indeed, progress was such that the Communist model was held-up as an example of how to do it. Strong economic progress continued after Stalin's death and by the 1960s the country was ready to make the transition to the Household stage.

The problem was that the Soviet leadership were thoroughly indoctrinated Stalinists, and they could not get their minds around the need to reform their economy. They were reluctant to shift away from the Urban stage habits of urban construction and heavy engineering projects. After all, those habits had worked so well for them that the country was now a rival superpower to the United States. So they kept on building bridges, steel mills, dams and armaments factories. The workers, left out of all decision-making and expected to do what they were told, stopped trying. The Soviet Union disintegrated in 1990.

Not every failure to make the Urban-to-Household transition leads to something as dramatic as a Great Depression or the disintegration of an empire. Many countries simply stall somewhere between the two stages. This has happened so often that it has been given a name: the Middle Income Trap.[80] Many nations get stuck in the Middle Income Trap. Those which have include most of the countries of Latin America, North Africa, the Middle East and some in South East Asia. They get stuck because their government either does not recognise the need to realign its policies, or it has not the strength to do it.

Can China make the transition to the Household stage? There is cause for optimism that it will manage it well, but there is also cause for pessimism. In short, it could go either way. It could launch itself into another era of rapid growth which sees its per capita wealth rise to the level of the nations of Western Europe in thirty or so years, or it could stall in its progress and get stuck in the Middle Income Trap along with Brazil, Thailand, Algeria and a host of other nations.

The Case For A Successful Transition

The case for China making a relatively trouble-free transition from the Urban to the Household stage rests mainly on the fact that the country has been remarkably capable in meeting the many and varied economic challenges which have stood in its path over the last forty years. As a nation it has shown itself to have the adaptability to overcome all sorts of obstacles which have stood in the way of its progress. The transition to the Household stage is, it could be said, just another challenge which will be overcome.

There is plenty of evidence to support this case because China's economic achievement since 1980 has been without precedent. There have been other large countries which have grown their economies very rapidly from a low base - Japan, South Korea and the Soviet Union are chief among them – but none have matched the performance of China. It has in just 40 years gone from being one of the poorest countries to being a middle-income nation with the largest economy in the world.

The post-Mao leadership deserves a good part of the credit. They recognised that the problems holding back the economy were mostly self-inflicted. So they set about unwinding the Mao-era policies which had been put in place to limit freedom of action. The reforms they enacted allowed the Chinese people to use their own capabilities to improve their own circumstances.

There were eight key reforms which, taken together, achieved this:

- *1979-83*: the Household Responsibility System, which broke-up the Agricultural Communes and returned the nation back to its proven system of family-run farms.
- *1980-84*: the establishment of Special Economic Zones which offered tax breaks and other inducements to attract foreign manufacturers to establish factories in selected coastal cities.
- *1982-84*: the unofficial relaxation of the *hukou* policy. This meant that China's legions of underemployed rural workers were given unofficial permission to travel to the large towns and cities to work in factories and on construction sites.
- *1984-86*: the introduction of a system whereby promotion for Communist Party officials was pegged to the economic performance of their region. This ensured that municipal

governments were geared up to push economic development as hard as they could.

- *1984-88* and *1992-96*: the removal of price controls on nearly all agricultural and manufactured products, and the establishment of a market economy.
- *1992-94*: the reform of the taxation system to restore the flow of tax revenues to the central government. By allowing municipal governments to lease the land which was under their control, it had the unintended consequence of providing a greatly increased revenue stream for cities and towns, which they used to build essential infrastructure.
- *1997-99*: privatisation of the social welfare responsibilities of the state-owned enterprises, including health, education and housing. This was another reform whose major benefit was an unintended consequence. In this case the sale of government housing led to a housing construction boom on a scale never before seen anywhere in the world.
- *1998-2001*: restructure of China's foreign trade rules to allow it entry into the World Trade Organisation.

China's economic progress could not have happened at the speed which it did without the migration of manufacturing businesses from Hong Kong and Taiwan to the mainland. It also greatly benefitted from the fact that major western economies were prepared to allow an almost unhindered inflow of Chinese-manufactured goods.

In another way of putting it, China's economic miracle was due to the fact that it was a politically stable country where there was a progressive liberation of the long-suppressed entrepreneurial capabilities of the common people. These capabilities were harnessed and guided by motivated local authorities who made it their business to:

- attract and promote industrial and commercial projects, both domestic and foreign, and
- assist them with modern infrastructure to become reliable exporters to developed country markets.

Which brings us to the present. China now needs to continue these reforms to bring it into the Household stage of economic development. According the framework which has just been discussed, the reforms now required have to be aimed at (1) gaining substantial increases in worker productivity and (2) achieving a more equitable distribution of the wealth which flows from these productivity gains.

One of the reasons for having confidence that China can implement these reforms is that the central government has clearly recognised them as being needed. This is shown in the Five Year Plans. The 12th Five Year Plan, announced in 2011, had two main priorities. The first was to focus the economy towards household consumption. The second was to upgrade the nation's skills, knowledge and infrastructure so as to support high tech industry. The 13th Five Year Plan, announced in 2016, was more specific. Household consumption was to be raised by bridging the "welfare gap" (meaning income inequality) between town and countryside. The shift to higher productivity industry would be achieved via a program called "Made in China 2025".[82]

A second reason for confidence is that China has, as of 2020 at least, a well-entrenched national government which has a strong hold over the reins of policy and power. And a third reason for confidence is that the reforms needed are by no means beyond the capability of a nation which has lifted itself so rapidly and decisively out of poverty and political extremism.

For a start, China already has nation-wide social security systems managing health care and employee welfare. There is a national pension scheme and a progressive income tax structure. As is to be expected in a country at China's stage of development, income distribution is skewed to the wealthy. According to the World Bank, in 2016 the country's GINI coefficient (a measure of income inequality where a higher score means greater inequality) was 38.5. This is high compared to China's industrialised neighbours – Japan, South Korea and Taiwan - and many Western European and South East Asian countries. But it is lower than the United States and nearly every country in Latin America. So China does not have an unusually high level of income inequality. Most of the inequality is due to the difference between urban and rural incomes, and coastal and inland provincial incomes. As more people leave the land and migrate to the coastal urban areas, this inequality is likely to reduce all by itself.

Two reforms would hasten this process. The first being the lifting of the *hukou* restrictions which continue to discourage migration from farm to city, and which make a permanent underclass of rural migrants living in the cities. The second is rural land reform. The average farm size in China remains at about one hectare, far lower than is warranted by modern farming equipment. Larger farms would push more people into the cities, raising the income levels of both those who depart for the cities and those who stay on the land. If the Chinese leadership chose to move, both of these reforms could be enacted at some time in the next decade or so.

A final reason for confidence is that the task facing China has been achieved by three of its near neighbours. Japan, South Korea and Taiwan have all passed through the Urban stage and then made the transition to the Household stage. In each case it was done with little in the way of societal upheaval. Japan did it in the 1960s, Taiwan in the 1980s and South Korea in the 1990s. These countries all have a cultural background somewhat similar to China, which suggests that Chinese society may well respond similarly to the challenges of the transition.

Taking all of the above, it is possible to form an optimistic view of China's future economic prospects. China appears to have the right mix of policies and capabilities to launch itself into the Household stage in the next five years or so. If it does that, there is every reason to expect that the economy will progress such that by the 2050s it will complete the Household stage and enter the ranks of the Advanced Countries, alongside its East Asian neighbours.

The Obstacles

It is also possible to form a quite different view of China's future. In another way of looking at it, China's economy and its government have many characteristics will which act to prevent it from achieving the transition. In this scenario, China will end up, as many nations have before it, stuck in the Middle Income Trap, permanently behind its wealthier neighbours.

There are five main obstacles standing in the way.

1 The economy is too dependent on urban stage construction

It will be recalled that the Soviet Union collapsed largely because it had become too comfortable with its Urban stage economic model of building more apartment blocks, factories, power stations, mines, roads, bridges, dams, irrigation networks and other engineering projects. It was the easy thing to do rather than tackle difficult reforms which would propel it into a new stage of economic growth.

China is showing signs of that same preference. For the past ten years it has stayed in its economic comfort zone despite clear signs, and clear acknowledgement in its own Five Year Plans, that it needs to shift into another mode of operation. The Urban stage habit of mind still prevails in much of China.

One example of this is the Ghost City. To define that term, a Ghost City is one which has been fully constructed but which has no inhabitants. These have now been part of the Chinese economic landscape for about 8 years, first appearing in any number in the years after the Global Financial Crisis, when China started living off debt-financed construction.

It is an established fact that many Ghost Cities do get filled up with inhabitants eventually. That said, the practice of building residential properties well in advance of when they will be occupied is a telling sign that there is not much else to do with the money, labour and materials which go into the cities. They are make-work projects of the kind which President Roosevelt would have liked to have been able to mobilise during the Great Depression.

2 There has been a withdrawal of international support

Although it is a Communist country, China has for a long time been given a lot of leeway by the Advanced Countries when it came to using trade to further its own economic development. The United States and the European Union have permitted large trade deficits to develop with China, presumably with the expectation that over time it would reciprocate by allowing US and EU services companies free access to China. This reciprocal access has not happened and now the wealthy countries are pushing back with tariffs and other trade restrictions. The firmest pushback is coming from the US which has long been the most generous towards China.

Given its rather privileged trade position, China's approach to its trading partners has been hard to understand. It has aggressively moved into the South China Sea claiming highly-questionable ownership rights over the open seas and establishing naval bases to enforce those claims. These are moves certain to antagonise the United States and the European Union as well as the countries of the region. It has also broken accepted rules of trade and is suspected of engaging in cyber crimes involving theft of data and industrial secrets.

Little wonder that it is losing the support of its main customers. This is not a good outcome for China. Japan, South Korea and Taiwan all retained trade support from the western countries as they moved into the Household stage, and this support was crucial in helping those countries in that effort. Without US and EU support, China's task becomes significantly more difficult.

3 Population growth is very low and the size of the active workforce is falling

From a demographic standpoint, China is now at the stage where Japan was in 1995. And in 1995, Japan had long completed its Household stage of development. In other words, China's demographic decline is coming very early on its industrialisation pathway. Its workforce is already in decline, and its total population will be in decline by 2030.

Like the withdrawal of international support, this is not a good outcome for China. This is because a growing population, and especially a growing workforce, is a strong driver of economic growth. Particularly when that population is relatively wealthy and well-educated. China benefitted greatly from the demographic engine driving the economy in the 1980s and 90s. Now it is gone, and gone with it (to an extent anyway) is the creativity which the younger members of the workforce bring. Other countries, the United States in particular, have turned to immigration to provide this engine of growth. This is unlikely to happen in China, and the result will be that its demographic decline will make it significantly more difficult for China to make the transition to the Household stage.

4 The great reformers have departed the scene

In the first section of this chapter were listed the eight important reforms which lifted the Chinese economy from poverty to prosperity. The most recent was the re-setting of trade rules which culminated in China's entry to the World Trade Organisation. That was completed in 2001, 20 years ago. There have been no reforms of real substance since then.

A common judgement made about the tenure of Hu Jintao and Wen Jiabao, who led China during 2003 to 2013, was that they neglected the reform agenda. That is overly critical because some reforms were implemented, mostly of an incremental nature such as expanding existing programs. But the big reforms, of the kind advanced by Zhao Zhiyang in the 1980s and then by Zhu Rongji in the 1990s, were not taken on. Neither have they been taken on by Xi Jinping and his deputy. The centrepiece of their tenure has been the anti-corruption campaign.

Yet there are a suite of big reforms still waiting to be tackled, among the most important:

- **Judicial independence,** this would end the current, conflicted system where the Communist Party is judge, jury and prosecutor.
- **Land reform,** which would allow China's small farm plots (which average about one hectare per family) to be consolidated, thereby increasing efficiency and yields, and allowing hundreds of millions of farm workers to shift to the urban areas and do more productive work.
- **Ending the *hukou* policy** which restricts movement of workers and their families across the country. By lifting these restrictions, and extending social security benefits to all "migrants" living in cities, a few hundred million urban families will be brought into the mainstream of Chinese economic life.
- **Merit-based financial lending** which would bring a lot of financially-strong, private-sector projects into being.

Instead of reforms, there have been two huge stimulus packages: the post-GFC rescue package and the Belt and Road initiative. These have not advanced the prospect of China moving into the Household stage. Quite the opposite, they have kept the current Urban stage economic model going, and further entrenched it.

5 The Communist Party is becoming more authoritarian

This is the biggest obstacle in the way of China moving on with its economic development. Authoritarian government is an untested quality when it comes to countries moving to the Household stage of development. So far, only liberal democracies have made the transition. Yet there is no logic which leads to the conclusion that an authoritarian government will be unable to lead its country through the transition. It depends upon how it uses its power.

The tolerant and open-to-ideas authoritarianism of Deng Xiaoping, Jiang Zemin and Hu Jintao would have placed no obstacle in the path of economic progress. The key issue is not whether a country's ruling party is authoritarian or democratically-elected, it is whether it is responsive to the needs of the people. The Chinese Communist Party has been responsive to the needs of the people since the beginning of the reform era in the late 1970s and this is a big part of why China has succeeded in the way that it has.

With the China's current leader, Xi Jinping, the governing style has shifted from tolerant to controlling. Where once the Communist Party was a broad church capable of assimilating a wide range of views, today it is being pushed into toeing the Party line without much discussion. This spells trouble for China because instituting tighter controls over the common people is not the way to make a successful transition from Urban to Household stage.

The Middle Income Trap Beckons

China is now in the firm grip of Xi Jinping, its fifth paramount leader. The first four, in order, were Mao Zedong, Deng Xiaoping, Jiang Zemin and Hu Jintao. Mao led the country for the best part of thirty years. The next three each served two five-year terms. This was not a co-incidence. Early in the Deng era, a constitutional amendment was passed that obliged the President to retire after serving two five-year terms. This retirement would, by convention, also require him to retire from his other top posts. This was adhered to Deng, Jiang and Hu. But it is not to be so with Xi Jinping. At the Party conference in 2017, the term-limit provision was scrapped. The post of President, and also that of vice-President, can now be held by the same person for an unlimited number of terms. The result is that Xi has become China's President for as long as he wants the job, and as long as he can hold onto it. History suggests that he will be in power for twenty plus years, taking his tenure well into the 2030s. That means that his policy preferences will determine China's future more or less to 2050.

What are his policy preferences? He favours the state-owned enterprise over private enterprise, and social stability and order over economic reform.[83] He seems unlikely to favour major reform if it brings with it the significant risk of widespread or unpredictable social disruption.

Xi has taken a widely-publicised and aggressive stand against corruption by Party officials. He has three aims with this. The first is to rehabilitate the image of the Communist Party and cause it to be seen once more as a force for good in society rather than a rapacious rent-seeker abusing its power over the common people. The second is to boost economic activity by removing this corruption and the costs it imposes on businesses. The third is to benefit himself by creating an image as a protector of the common people while at the same time removing his rivals, most of whom are vulnerable because virtually every senior Chinese official would have committed prosecutable corruption at, as a minimum, some time in their careers.

The anti-corruption campaign is one of the bright spots in Xi Jinping's policymaking to date. Another is his attempts to eradicate poverty although this seems to remain mostly in the realm of good intentions. Beyond that, however, there is not much being done to foster a higher productivity workforce which has a greater share in national wealth. Little, if any, effort has been put into the necessary reforms of land ownership, bank lending, the judiciary and the *hukou* policy. Instead there is a continuation of Urban stage economic policies: more government money is being lent to government-owned companies who spend it on infrastructure projects of questionable value.

If China is to make the shift to the Household stage, Xi Jinping's administration needs to be far more active in unlocking the potential of its people. Instead, it is at its most active when locking down the potential of its people. It does this by demanding strict adherence to Party-mandated behaviours and beliefs and instituting programs of mass surveillance. This is to say nothing of the repressive measures taken against its enemies such Muslim Uighurs and Falun Gong. These measures may, in the end, have little impact on economic behaviour but at the very least they are diverting government focus from the real issues facing the economy.

The management of the economy in China of the 2020s is looking like the Soviet Union of the 1970s. Major reforms and a shift of official mindset are needed to keep the economy moving along the path of progress. But, as in the Soviet Union, China finds itself in an economic comfort zone in which its leaders prefer to remain rather than risk the turmoil which accompanies the necessary reforms. The Middle Income Trap beckons.

References

1. *Third Plenary Session of the Eleventh Central Committee of the CPC held in 1978,* People's Daily On-Line, 9 October 2008
2. *China's Global Role,* John Franklin Copper, Hoover Institution Press, Stanford University. 1980.
3. *China's industrial growth 1953-57,* Ronald Hsia, The Annals of the American Academy of Political and Social Science, Vol 321, 1959
4. *Collectivisation and China's Agricultural Crisis in 1959-61,* Justin Yifu Lin, Journal of Political Economy, Vol 98, 1990
5. *The Chinese People's Communes and the Modernisation of Agriculture,* Manfred Romich, China Report, Vol 17, 1981
6. *The Great Leap Forward: Anatomy of a Central Planning Disaster,* Dennis Tao Yang and Wei Li, Journal of Political Economy, Vol 113, 2005
7. *The Great Sparrow Campaign was the start of the greatest mass starvation in history,* John Platt, Mother Nature Network, 30 September 2013
8. *Causes, Consequences and Impact of the Great Leap Forward in China,* Hsiung-Shen Jung and Jui Lung-Chen, Asian Culture and History, Vol 11, 2019
9. *Mao's Great Famine: the history of China's most devastating catastrophe,* Frank Dikötter, Bloomsbury, 2010
10. *Deng Xiaoping: A Revolutionary Life,* Alexander Pantsov and Steven Levine, Oxford University Press, 2015
11. *Unlikely Partners: Chinese Reformers, Western Economists and the making of global China,* p20, Julian Gerwitz, Harvard University Press, 2017
12. *Dealing with responsibility for the Great Leap Famine in the People's Republic of China,* Felix Wemheuer, The China Quarterly, No 201, 2010

13. *The Cultural Revolution: A People's History 1962-1976*, Frank Dikötter, Bloomsbury, 2016
14. *Mao's Cultural Revolution: The Struggle to Consolidate Power*, Paul Bridgham, China Quarterly, No 41, 1970
15. *Deng Xiaoping and the Transformation of China*, Ezra F Vogel, Belknap Press, 2013
16. *China's coup of October 1976*, Keith Forster, Modern China, Vol 18, 1992
17. *An analysis of China's grain production: looking backward and forward*, Weifeng Zhang et al, Food and Energy Security, 2014
18. *Public sector housing in urban China 1949-1988: the case of Xian*, Ya Ping Wang, Housing Studies, Vol 10, 1995
19. *Reflections on forty years of China's reforms*, Bret Hofman, World Bank, speech at Fudan University, January 2018
20. *Chinese Politics: The Fall of Hua Kuo-Feng to the Twelfth Party Congress*, ed James T Myers, University of South Carolina Press, 1995
21. *The End of China's One-Child Policy*, Wang Feng et al, Studies in Family Planning, Brookings Institution, 2016
22. *How the farmers changed China: Power of the People*, Kate Xiao Zhou, Westview Press, 1996
23. *Agricultural reform in China: from Communes to Commodity Economy, 1978-1990*, Simon Powell, Manchester University Press
24. *Town and Village Enterprises in China*, Xiaolan Fu and VN Balasubramanyam, Journal of development Studies, vol 39, 2003
25. *Rural Reform and Social Change in the Countryside*, Wang Xiaoyi, chapter 2 in Thirty Years of Reform and Social Change in China, edited by Li Qiang, Brill 2010
26. *Hong Kong: The Ongoing Economic Miracle*, Jean-Francois Minardi, Montreal Economic Institute, 2013
27. *Shenzhen, China Metro Area Population, 1950-2010*, United Nations – World Population Prospects, 2020
28. *Shenzhen, a Chinese development zone in global perspective*, Leslie Sklair, Development and Change, Vol 16, 2008, also
    a. *China's Special Economic Zones and Industrial Clusters: Success and Challenges*, Douglas Zeng, Working Paper, Lincoln Institute of Land Policy, 2012
    b. *China's Special Economic Zones: Five Years After*, Chung-Tong Wu, Asian Journal of Public Administration, 1985

c. *An Assessment of China's Special Economic Zones,* Karen McKenney, National Defence University, Washington DC. April 1993

d. *The Special Economic Zones of China and their Impact on its Economic Development,* Jung-Dong Park, Praeger 1997

29. *Yao Yilin, A Hundred-Night Talk,* Yao Jin, Communist Party History Publishing House, 2008

30. *Proximity and Complementarity in Hong Kong-Shenzhen Industrialisation,* Weiping Wu, Asian Survey, Vol XXXVII, No 8, August 1997

31. *The Chinese Economy: International Trade,* Lecture 9 of the "China, Hong Kong and the World Economy" Course, Department of Economics, Lingnan University, 29 July 2018

32. *State-owned Enterprise Reform in China, Past, Present and Prospects,* Ligang Song, from the book China's Forty Years of Reform and Development. ANU Press 2018

33. *Selected Works of Deng Xiaoping, Volume II (1975-1982),* complied by Deng Xiaoping, Deng Xiaoping Works, 1995

34. *Contract Responsibility System: Transition from a Planned to a Market Economy,* Anthony YC Koo, Economic Development and Cultural Change, Vol 38, 1990

35. *The Dual Pricing System in China's Industry,* Wu Jingliang and Zhu Renwei, Journal of Comparative Economics, Vol 11 1987

36. *Reforms in China: Problems and Prospects,* Lev P Deliusin, Asian Survey, Vol 28, 1988

37. *China – the Tienanmen Square Massacre of 1989,* M Anne Brown, Chapter 4 in Human rights and the borders of suffering, Manchester University Press, 2002

38. *Hu Yaobang, A Chinese Biography,* Yang Zhongmei, ME Sharpe, 1988

39. *Tienanmen Square protest death toll was "about 10,000",* report on BBC, 23 December 2017

40. *Prisoner of the State: the secret journal of Premier Zhao Zhiyang,* Zhao Zhiyang, Simon and Schuster, 2009

41. *China since Tienanmen: the Politics of Transition,* Joseph Fewsmith, Cambridge University Press, 2012

42. *Deng Xiaoping's Southern Tour: Elite Politics in post-Tienanmen China,* Suisheng Zhou, Asian Survey, Vol 33, 1993

43. *A look back at Deng Xiaoping's speech in southern China two decades ago,* He Qinglian, 19 January 2012

44. *China's transition to a market economy: how far across the river?,* Yingyi Qian and Jinglian Wu, Working Paper No. 69, Department of Economics, Stanford University, May 2000
45. *The History of Taiwan,* Bruce Jacobs, The China Journal, January 2011
46. *The Taiwanese Economy after the Miracle,* Philippe Chevalerias, China Perspectives, 2010/3, also
    a. *Industrial agglomeration of Hong Kong and Taiwanese manufacturing investment in China: a town-level study of Dongguan,* Chun Yang and Haifeng Liao, 23 May 2009, The Annals of Regional Science
47. *The nature and trend of Taiwanese investment in China (1991 to 2014),* Chung-Min Tsai, from the book China and Taiwan, University of California Press 2017
48. *The Chinese Economy under Deng Xiaoping,* edited by Robert Ash and YY Kueh, Clarendon Press, 1996
49. *China embraces the market,* Department of Foreign Affairs and Trade (Australia), 1997
50. *China's Hukou Reform and the Urbanization Challenge,* Spencer Sheehan, 22 February 2017
51. *Surplus Rural Labourers and Internal Migration in China: Current Status and Future Prospects,* Cheng Li, Asian Survey, November 1996, also
    a. *Urbanisation, Agriculture and Industrialisation in China, 1952-91,* Denise Young and Honghai Deng, Urban Studies, Vol 35, 1998
52. *Regional Powerhouse: The Greater Pearl River Delta and the Rise of China,* Michael Enright et al, Wiley, 2005
53. *Breaking the iron Rice Bowl: Evidence of Precautionary Savings from the Chinese State-Owned Companies Reform,* Hui He et al, Working Paper 04-2014, Federal Reserve Bank of San Francisco, 2014, also
    a. *China in 1995: Mounting Problems, Waning Capacity,* John Bryan Starr, Asian Survey Vol 6, Jan 1996
54. *Zhu Rong-Ji on the Record: The Road to Reform, 1998-2003,* Zhu Rong-Ji, Brookings Institution Press, 2015
    a. *The Origins of Successful Economic Reform in China,* Ross Garnaut, Research School of Pacific and Asian Studies, Australian National University, paper presented at China Centre for Economic Research, Peking University, 16-17 September 2004
    b. *The Real Reasons for China's Growth,* Wing Thye Woo, The China Journal, January 1999

55. *Pudong – Another Special Economic Zone in China,* Bin Xue Sang, Northwestern Journal of International Law and Business, Fall 1993

56. *Economic Reform and Growth in China,* Gregory C Chow, Annals of Economic and Finance, 2004

57. *Understanding China's Growth: Past, Present and Future,* Xiaodong Zhu, Journal of Economic Perspectives, Fall 2012

58. *China's Rapid Growth and Development: An Historical and International Context,* Ligang Song, from China's New Role in the World Economy, 2013

59. *Housing Improvement and Distribution in Urban China: Initial Evidence from China's 2000 Census,* Wang Feng, China Review, Fall 2003

60. *From welfare housing to the home ownership: the dilemma of China's housing reform,* James Lee, Housing Studies, Vol 15, 2000

    a. *Household Consumption Trends in China,* Mark Baker and David Osmond, Reserve Bank Bulletin, March Quarter 2010

    b. *Housing reform and home ownership behaviour in China,* Michael Ho and Tsz-Man Kwong, Housing Studies, Vol 17, 2002

    c. *Housing reform and its impacts on the urban poor in China,* Ya Ping Wang, Housing Studies, Vol 15, 2000

61. *The winners in China's urban housing reform,* John Logan, Yiping Fang and Zhanxin Zhang, Housing Studies, No.1, January 2010

62. *Demystifying the Chinese Housing Boom,* Hanming Fang et al, National Bureau of Economic Research, 2016

63. *Housing reform and the housing market in China,* Yang Z. and Chen Y., Springer Publishing, 2014

64. *Regional Powerhouse: The Greater Pearl River Delta and the Rise of China,* Michael Enright et al, Wiley, 2005

65. *Global Capital, the State and Chinese Workers: the Foxconn Experience,* Pun Ngai and Penny Chan, Modern China, 2012

66. *China, International Trade and WTO Accession,* Thomas Rumbaugh and Nicolas Blancher, IMF March 2004

67. *Globalisation and the Shanghai Model: A Retrospective and Prospective Analysis,* Linsun Cheng, University of Massachusetts, Journal of International and Global Studies 4(1) 2012

68. *The Emergence of the Pearl River Delta Economic Zone,* Keiichiro Oizumi, Pacific and Business Industries, Vol 11, 2011

69. *National Bureau of Statistics of China,* data for years 2010 and 2000

70. *China as the World Factory*, edited by Kevin Honglin Zhang, Routledge, 2006
71. *China's Processing Trade: a firm level analysis*, Miaojie Wu and Wei Tian, from Rebalancing and Sustaining Growth in China, ANU Press 2012
72. *Infrastructure Investment in China*, Kelsey Wilkins and Andrew Zurawski, Reserve Bank of Australia June Quarter 2014, also
73. *Taxation and Economic Growth in China*, Roger Gordon and Wei Lee, May 2002
74. *China's Fiscal and Tax Reforms: a critical move on the chessboard*, Daniel H Rosen, Rhodium Group, 2014
75. *China and the Global Economy*, Justin Yifu Lin, Asian Economic Policy Conference sponsored by Federal Reserve Bank of San Francisco, November 29-30, 2011
76. *Understanding the China Stimulus Package*, Barry Naughton, China Leadership Monitor, No 28
77. *The long shadow of China's fiscal expansion*, Chong-En Bai, Chang-Tai Hsieh, Zheng Song Brookings Papers on Economic Activity, Fall 2016
78. *Supporting China's Infrastructure Stimulus and the INFRA Platform*, INFRA Update June 2010, World Bank
79. *The Stages of Economic Growth: a Non-Communist Manifesto*, Walt Whitman Rostow, Cambridge University Press, 1960
80. *The Path of Industrialisation: 1880 to 2050*, Martin Lynch, InHousePublishing, 2021
81. *The Middle Income Trap: is there a way out for Asian countries?* Raisal Lubis and Putu Saputra, Journal of Indonesian Economy and Business, Vol 30, 2015
82. *Made in China 2025 Backgrounder*, Institute for Security and Development Policy, June 2018
83. *The Third Revolution: Xi Jinping and the New Chinese State*, Elizabeth C Economy, Oxford University Press, 2016

Made in the USA
Monee, IL
04 November 2026

67380388R00066